# Tea Bliss

# Tea Bliss

Infuse Your Life with Health,
Wisdom, and Contentment

Theresa Cheung

Conari Press

First published in 2007 by Conari Press,
an imprint of Red Wheel/Weiser, LLC
With offices at:
500 Third Street, Suite 230
San Francisco, CA 94107
*www.redwheelweiser.com*

ISBN-10: 1-57324-211-X
ISBN-13: 978-1-57324-211-0
Library of Congress Cataloging-in-Publication Data is available upon request

Cover and text design by Donna Linden.
Typeset in High Society and Bembo.
All photographs © Creatas unless otherwise noted. Cover and page 105 photograph
© Corbis; pages 37, 59, and 130 © Janis Christie/Photodisc Inc.; pages 77, 90, and 134
© Allison Miksch/Brand X Pictures.

Printed in Hong Kong
SS
10  9  8  7  6  5  4  3  2  1

# Contents

# Acknowledgments

A big thank you to Jan Johnson, Caroline Pincus, Jordan Overby and everyone at Red Wheel for their vision and encouragement and for allowing me to combine two of my passions: tea and writing. Special thanks to Donna Linden for her inspirational designs and Brenda Knight for her editorial guidance. Finally, thank you Ray, Robert, and Ruth for your love, support, and patience as I went into self-imposed exile to complete this project.

# Introduction

## *finding peace in a bowl of tea*

Savor the moment, says tea; appreciate me for what I am. Calm down and drink me; life is too precious to waste. Wait for me to steep, delight in my fragrance, and watch the steam rise from my cup. Appreciate your friends, or the silence reflecting your thoughts. When you are ready, take a sip, feel the glow of my sweet warmth, and make a wish.

A cup of tea is the perfect excuse to step back and savor life as it should be lived, moment by moment. Finding peace in a bowl of tea isn't new—the sublime art of tea drinking has been practiced in Asia for centuries—but its wisdom is timeless. It represents a universal path to inner peace and enlightenment that is just as potent today as it has always been.

I love tea for the refreshing effect it has not just on my taste buds but also on my spirit. When life feels overwhelming, just one sip of warm tea down my throat and the whole world loosens up. A cup of tea in the morning sets the pace for the day. Sitting and chatting with a few good friends over a couple of rounds of tea makes life worth living. Nothing gives me more pleasure than sampling new teas and finding new tastes to suit every mood and occasion. With its subtly changing color, taste, and aroma, tea is an endless source of comfort, inspiration, and romance.

It was after a particularly satisfying cup of tea at the end of a long and stressful day that I started to think about the drink I was holding in my hand. Some people search for a lifetime to find enlightenment. Tea masters find it in the everyday, the here and now—in every breath, in every cup of tea. Is it possible, I wondered, for all of us to find peace in a bowl of tea?

The nourishing blends for health, happiness, and harmony you'll find in this book are as simple, refreshing, comforting, and enlightening as the beverage that inspired them. There is nothing complicated, antiquated, or ambiguous here. Whether you are passionate about tea or simply enjoy it from time to time, you will find here positive reflections, practical strategies, and inspirational techniques that can help you feel healthier and happier and at peace with yourself and the world—right here, right now, this moment in your daily life. As you read, never forget that tea is more than just a drink; it's a state of mind, a way of life. Savor the moment, says tea; appreciate me for what I am. Discover in me the truth of the universe. Be surprised by the magic I can help you discover within yourself.

*Find yourself a cup; the teapot is behind you. Now tell me a hundred things.*
—Saki (1870–1916), British writer

# Ten Nourishing Blends for Health, Happiness, and Harmony

1. Discover the right measure.
   *Give what you want to receive.*
2. Boiling is not always best.
   *Put away your to-do list at some time every day.*
3. Know what's in the water.
   *Become aware of your unique talents and potential.*
4. Choose the right teapot.
   *Develop a sound philosophy.*
5. Make sure the taste is evenly distributed.
   *Find the right middle way.*
6. Time is of the essence.
   *Enjoy today, but keep an eye on tomorrow.*
7. Make and serve a delicious cup of tea.
   *Put your heart into everything you do.*
8. Healing with tea
   *Bring healing into your life.*
9. Meditate with tea.
   *Find your path to inner peace.*
10. Cultivate the tea mind.
    *Satisfy the spirits in your life.*

# Nourishing Blend № 1

## discover the right measure

About Tea: Brewing tea is a weighty exercise and always begins with a scale.

About Life: Give and receive in equal measure. Give what you want to receive, and always accept and return support.

For thousands of years, wise people have poured hot water over tea leaves and found pleasure in both the experience and the drink that is created. Referred to as the "agony of the leaves," the reaction of dried leaves to hot water can be a lovely thing to watch; it holds an almost poetic beauty, especially if you brew in a clear vessel and use larger-leafed teas such as oolong. And the resulting beverage is a truly great tea with an exceptional flavor, aroma, and color.

> *There is a great deal of poetry and fine sentiment in a chest of tea.*
> —Ralph Waldo Emerson (1803–1882), American poet and essayist

It's often thought that serving tea from loose leaves is too complicated or time consuming, but all you need to brew the perfect cup are three things—tea, hot water, and a vessel—and once you know a few simple rules, it is really quite simple. The first and possibly most important step is to get the balance between the water and tea leaves right.

Great brewing begins with a scale. It's the same in life. You need to find the right balance between giving and taking. For happy, contented living, you need to understand that your ability to give and to receive lies at the core of your ability to create and experience true prosperity.

> *"Tea and Water give each other life," the Professor was saying. "The tea is still alive. This tea has tea and water vitality," he added. . . . "Afterwards, the taste still happens. . . . It rises like velvet. . . . It is a performance."*
> —Jason Goodwin, *The Gunpowder Gardens*

## Getting the Balance Right

When you brew tea, make sure you get the balance right between tea and water. A standard cup of tea is around 5.5–liquid ounces, so you need to know the water capacity of your teapot, because this will determine how much tea you need to use. The general rule is to use 2 grams of tea leaves for every 5.5–liquid ounce cup of tea.

Taking time to get the balance of tea to water right will remind you of the importance of balancing giving with receiving in life. Giving and receiving are opposites that are linked together in the natural flow of life, just like breathing out and breathing in. If one aspect of that flow doesn't function, the life force is blocked. If you can't breathe in, you can't breathe out, and your body cannot continue living.

Last week at a friend's birthday party I started chatting with a woman I hadn't met before. Noticing how busy the party was, she jokingly said that nobody ever remembered her birthday but that it was her own fault because she never remembered anyone else's. Looking over at the birthday girl chatting and laughing happily, I

# The One True Leaf

The tea leaf comes from an evergreen, perennial shrub called *Camellia sinensis,* a distant relative of the showy, shiny-leaved camellia that gardeners and landscapers love.

Tea plantations are typically calm and serene places. The smooth lines of slopes and hills are broken only by the undulations of shade-growing trees. Because tea is usually picked by hand, the only sounds rising from the bushes are the voices of pickers and the occasional distant hum of a van or tractor.

It takes about five years for tea bushes to develop, but after that they can be harvested for fifty or sixty years. The flavor of the harvested tea varies from day to day, depending on the weather, the soil, and the climate. That's why blends are important, as they ensure some form of consistency. There are several thousand varieties of tea, and they vary around the world even from valley to valley. If a tea bush is on a sunny slope, its leaves will taste different from the leaves of one that is on a shady slope.

Just the very tip and top leaves of each branch go into making the perfect cup, and the best-quality teas are still harvested by hand across the globe in India, Pakistan, Nepal, Sri Lanka, parts of Africa, and parts of South America. If tea is picked mechanically, the coarser leaves and stems are often picked along with the tender leaves. These coarser leaves are manufactured—cut, torn, and crushed—to create powder that will brew quickly and be used to make tea bags or instant tea.

thought about all the years I had known her and how in all that time she had never failed to offer her friendship and support when it was needed. I suspected that she was as generous with her other friends as she was with me, and today was our chance to support and cherish her. She was getting friendship from us by giving it first.

Quality tea shouldn't have too much or too little water. You need to get the proportions right. In life also you need to give and take in equal measure; you need to get the balance right. If you want to be loved, give love to others. If you want respect, give it to others. If you want to be supported, support others. If you want to share in the happiness of others, share your happiness and success. If you want to lift yourself up, the best way is to lift others up.

A wise tale:

*Two men were traveling together on a road. One of them found a purse lying by the side of the road. "Look!" he cried. "I'm so lucky. I've found a purse, and it's full of gold coins." And indeed, the purse was full of gold coins. "Shouldn't you say how lucky we are?" replied his companion. "I thought we were traveling together. I thought companions share everything." "Nice try," smiled the other man. "I found it, so it's mine to keep."*

*A little later they were stopped by a mob of angry people shouting, "Has anyone found a purse?" The man who had picked up the purse went pale with fright. "We are lost," he whispered to his companion. "If they find the purse on us, they will think we stole it. Help me hide it quickly before they reach us!" But his companion was not frightened. "Don't say we are lost," he said. "You would not say we before, so why say it now?"*

**Moral: If you do not share your success, do not expect others to share in your sorrows.**

The more you give, the happier you will become, not just because generosity brings other people closer to you and increases the likelihood that they will be there for you, but also because the good feeling that comes from the act of giving makes you feel good about yourself, and when you feel good about yourself, life automatically becomes smoother. Generosity's true reward is not a favor returned but the warmth and happiness you feel after you have given. Research even shows that regular volunteer work increases life expectancy, decreases boredom, and creates purpose in life. Volunteer workers are twice as likely to feel happy as nonvolunteers.

But shouldn't you give without wanting anything in return? If you give because you expect repayment, you are setting yourself up for unhappiness. Your attitude is crucial here: giving has to be motivated not by greed but by the true spirit of generosity. Give from your heart, not your head. Never give in order to manipulate; avoid giving if it is likely to cause you resentment; and never approach giving like a bookkeeper. The credit for your compassion may not show up for a long time, and it may never show up except in your heart.

Giving that is motivated by the true spirit of generosity is one of the fastest and most effective ways to feel better about yourself and your life. People who only take in life always end up lonely and miserable.

But, although giving is a vital ingredient for a happy life, Nourishing Blend #1 is all about getting the balance right. You need to be a giver, but you also need to be able to receive in equal measure. In theory this sounds simple, but, as we explore later, learning to give from the heart and receive with gratitude isn't as simple or as easy as it sounds.

*I always fear that creation will expire before teatime. Thank God for tea!*
—The Reverend Sidney Smith (1771–1845), English clergyman and writer

# Measuring Tea

Tea leaves often vary in size and weight, so it can be difficult to translate 2 grams into a measure such as a teaspoon. Try using an accurate gram scale along with measuring spoons, and discover what 2 grams of tea looks like in your spoon. So if it takes you $2^1/_2$ teaspoons to make 2 grams and you are using an 11-ounce teapot, then you will need 5 teaspoons to make a pot. It might be a good idea once you have found the right measure for a particular tea to record it so it's easier next time you measure out a pot of tea.

# Tea Bags

The tea bag was invented in 1908 by New Yorker Thomas Sullivan, who stitched up his tea samples into little silk sachets. He soon realized that they gave a quick strong brew and were much easier to use than loose leaves. In the intervening years tea bags have gone through many tweaks, changing from square to round to pyramid-shaped to oblong and back again. Today tea bags rule the world. There is no doubt that tea leaves are messy, and you may choose to avoid them by using tea bags. Tea in bags will never match the exquisite taste of loose leaves, but tea bags are incredibly convenient, and these days you are probably as likely to get a decent cup of tea out of a tea bag as out of loose tea.

If you've always used tea bags, why not try using leaves and a tea strainer for a few days? You'll notice the difference in taste immediately. And should you want to switch to tea leaves completely, hang on to those old tea bags. You can restore sparkle to sore eyes by placing cool stewed tea bags on closed eyelids.

If you decide to stick with tea bags because they are the quicker and easier option, make sure you don't lose the chance of taking a break from the stresses of daily life as you reflect over the kettle and the brewing tea.

## Do Small Things with Great Love

Loving others and giving to them give us a feeling of self-worth because we are helping to make the world a better place. Giving fills our lives with meaning. It sounds easy, doesn't it? But, unless you are Mother Teresa, balancing your desire to please yourself with giving to others is likely to be a struggle. Unfortunately, we tend to spend far too much effort on being loved, being respected, being seen in the right places and with the right people. We obsess about what to say, what to wear, what to drive—all things that have to do with getting others to like us rather than thinking about how we can help others. But there is something even greater than being loved, even greater than fulfilling our ambitions. What is that? It is going out of our way to be of assistance to others. It is being a giver.

The elaborate ritual of the Japanese tea ceremony can teach us much about the art of giving. This ceremony represents the culmination of the Japanese elevation of tea from a drink and a medicine to a way or philosophy of life. The ceremony is still practiced today all over the world, and even if you do not want to embrace tea as a religion or philosophy, there is beauty in the practice and much to be learned from the tea state of mind. The tea ceremony cultivates qualities such as loving attention to every detail, however small, focusing solely on the task in hand, and being completely dedicated, as a host, to giving every consideration to those with whom you find yourself.

*Tea is the beverage of ceremonious people, and like the dense monsoon rains, it is both calming and stimulating, encouraging conversation and relaxation. Ideas and traditions steep slowly in its steamy transparence.*
—Pascal Bruckner, contemporary French novelist

Here are some suggestions to help you shift into more giving behavior:

- Have you ever woken up and felt really stressed and tired and then, when you went out, someone gave you a cheery smile or stepped aside so that you could go first, and suddenly the world seemed a bit brighter? Every morning, promise to do at least one thing that will make someone else feel good and you feel good about yourself: Offer a compliment; make tea for a friend; drop off some flowers to a hospital with a request that they be given to someone who doesn't normally get visitors; call on an elderly neighbor for five minutes to make sure they are okay; let the person behind you in the supermarket with only a few items go ahead of you; if you are dining out, pile up your dishes neatly so that they will be easier for the waiter to clear; let a driver into the traffic; offer to babysit for a couple who doesn't get out much; give up your seat to someone who needs it; if you are working with someone, give them lots of thanks; give someone a compliment; hold the door open for the person behind you. The possibilities are endless.

- Don't talk negatively about other people. Stop discussing people you don't like, and if the subject comes up, always cast them in a positive light.
- Accept loving and generous behavior from others with gratitude. Other people have a need to give too. Letting others help you may make you feel vulnerable, but to get the balance right in your life you need to be receptive and spontaneous.
- Consider doing some regular volunteer work.
- Offer your help and support or comfort to those you care about when they are in need or down on their luck. This is often when most people need support, but unfortunately it's also when most people desert them. If you can't offer practical help, give hope, friendship, or a confidence boost. This doesn't cost you much but is highly appreciated.
- When talking to people, take the time to really listen to what they have to say. Sometimes just sparing time and listening without interrupting or offering advice can be the greatest act of giving.
- Share the spotlight. Forget about your ego, and earn the respect of others by giving them credit when they deserve it. Share your ideas, and praise other people's efforts. Recognize other people,

and let them know how much you value them. This shows that you don't care about your ego; you care about the idea, the project, the relationship, the objective.

- Follow the Golden Rule, and treat others as you would want them to treat you. Think about what an offer of help means to someone else, not to you. If you have something nice to say, say it. Don't wait until people are dead to send them flowers. If you are concerned about feeling vulnerable, stop viewing relationships as a competition and see them more as a celebration. You don't win in relationships; you win by having relationships.

Think about what motivates you to give and what stops you from giving. Think about what kind of giving makes you feel good about yourself and what kind makes you feel resentful. Then think about what you would like to do to increase the giving behavior that makes you feel warm and comforted. Look each day for ways to perform random acts of kindness. Try it for a week, and notice how giving behavior not only makes you feel good but also brings you good fortune.

## Love Is Always Knocking on the Door

Let's return to the theme of balance. Yes, giving can boost your chances of happiness, but you need to balance giving with receiving. For a happy and contented life, you need to give and receive in equal measure.

You have probably heard at some time or another the advice that only after you love yourself can you love someone else. This applies to giving. Only after you know how to give to yourself, to accept support when it is offered, can you give it fully to others.

You may find it hard to accept generosity. Does it make you feel vulnerable? Perhaps you find it easier to be in the position of giver, creating indebtedness rather than feeling indebted. If this is the case, remember that it isn't all about you. Other people have just as much need to give love and help as you do. Why not let other people feel good about themselves by receiving and being grateful when help is offered to you?

If you give too much and don't take care of yourself or accept support when it is offered, your chances of happiness, health, and success in life are minimized. Think about it: if you aren't open to love, good fortune, and happiness, how can they ever find you?

If you have problems with receiving, ask yourself why and how you are blocking good things, like love, friendship, generosity, and support from coming to you. Why do you prefer to be self-sufficient? What happened to you to make you shun help when it is offered? What short-term benefit does shutting off from others give you?

Why is it so hard for you to open up and ask for help or friendship? What can you do today to open yourself more to receiving love, support, and help from other people? The universe rewards an open hand more than a closed fist. Love is always knocking on the door, but it won't come to you unless you open to it and are willing to let it in.

*A preacher finds himself caught in a tremendous rainstorm, and within a few hours the motel he is staying in is flooded. As the water rises, he climbs on the roof and starts praying. Just then a rescue party floats by in a rowing boat. "Let's go, mister. Get into the boat."*

*"I'll stay here," says the preacher. "The Lord will save me."*

*Two hours later a second boat reaches the motel. "You better get in! The water is rising still."*

*"No thanks," says the preacher. "The Lord will save me."*

*Toward evening the motel is almost completely under water and the preacher is clinging to the satellite dish on the roof. Another boat passes by. "Hey, buddy, get in the boat. This is your last chance."*

*"I'm all right," says the preacher, looking toward heaven. "I know the Lord will save me."*

*As the boat departs, the satellite dish is hit by lightning and the preacher is killed. When he arrives at the pearly gates he is furious. "What happened?" he shouts. "I thought the Lord would provide."*

*Within seconds a thunderous reply is heard. "Give me a break, pal. I sent three boats."*

## Don't Forget to Fill Your Own Cup

Common sense and scientific research agree that until you have met your own physical and emotional needs, you can't muster sufficient resources for someone else. When you start to neglect yourself for the sake of other people, you simply can't be effective in helping them.

To live a happy, contented life you need a giving nature, but you also need self-love. Give to others, by all means, but not to the point that your own needs are neglected. Just as the only way to know if the tea you are serving to your guests is of the right quality is to taste and enjoy it yourself first, you need to consider yourself as well—not just as an afterthought, but all the time.

Happy, healthy people have learned how important self-care is for their well-being, so they integrate it in their lives. There are lots of ways to take care of yourself, and in Nourishing Blend #2—Boiling is not always best—you'll find plenty of suggestions that have been supported by scientific research as surefire ways to boost your chances of health and happiness.

## The Right Chemistry

Quality tea is a matter of chemistry. When you brew tea, you are trying to get the perfect balance between hot water and tea. To live a contented life, you also need to find the right balance between giving and receiving. How will you know when you are getting this balance right? You'll know because life starts to get easier. Your struggles don't disappear, but you feel better able to manage them. There is more flow and balance in your life, and every now and again you experience something amazing called *synergy*.

If you have ever watched a flock of geese heading south for the winter flying in a V-formation, or listened to a great orchestra, you've seen synergy. If you've ever been on a team of any kind, you've felt synergy. If you've ever worked on a project that really came together or been out with a group of good friends and had a fantastic time, you've experienced it.

Synergy is achieved when people work together to create a better solution than any one of them could have achieved alone. Have you ever found that something that seemed impossible suddenly seemed easier to cope with when you talked about it with a friend? You share your point of view, get your friend's point of view, and suddenly see things in a new way. This is the magic of synergy.

Synergy is the perfect balance between give and take. It's not about your way but about a better way, a higher way. A good band is a great example of synergy. It's not just the drums, the guitar, the vocalist, or the piano; it's about everyone working together to make music. Each band member brings his or her strengths to the band. No member is more important than another. Each one blends with the others to create something better than she or he would achieve alone.

It isn't always easy working toward synergy. Synergy doesn't just happen; it's a process, and you have to help it along with a lot of give and take. You get there by opening your mind, sharing your point of view, and listening to and understanding the points of view of others. You get there by working together to find solutions that are positive for everyone, including you. You get there by giving from the heart and being open to what others have to give you. Synergy is the magic happening. If you are sharing your journey, you can create things more wonderful than you ever could have alone.

Think again of that band or, if you prefer, an orchestra. Individually the voices and instruments make different sounds and pause at

# The Perfect Brew

1. Empty your kettle of any leftover water, and fill with freshly drawn cold water. Let the tap run for a little while before you fill the kettle. Never use hot water from the tap. Filtered and bottled water are both less oxygenated than water from the tap, so use them only if your tap water is poor quality. Let the kettle boil, but boil the water only once. Overboiled or reboiled water has lost much of its oxygen and makes for a very dull cup.
2. Warm your pot, mug, bowl, or cup by filling it up with hot water. If the pot, mug, or bowl is too cold, this will reduce the temperature of the boiling water when it is poured in. Discard this water when the kettle boils.
3. Measure in your tea. A tea bag contains 2.25 grams of tea and a teaspoon 5 to 8 grams.
4. If you are having black tea, pour the water into the mug, cup, bowl, or pot as it boils. Water that isn't boiling won't be hot enough. If you're having green tea, wait a few moments before you pour.
5. Leave to infuse for a few minutes.
6. Linger over your drink, and enjoy the break from routine. Many specialty teas have very subtle differences that are easily ignored if you make tea in haste.

different times, yet they aren't competing with one another but working and blending together to create a harmony. Think again of the importance of balancing giving and taking in your life. Giving to and supporting others creates good feeling and warmth in yourself and others, but for true happiness you also need to be able to receive love and support. Think again of your tea. Individually the water and the tea can't work their magic, but blend them together, get the balance just right, and you are on your way to making the perfect brew.

## Milk in First or Second?

The correct way is to put the milk in first because the hot tea homogenizes the fats in the milk. However, this only works if you know exactly how strong your brew is and how much milk you will need. Pouring the tea first may have originated as a way to show off the quality of one's china and the brew itself. In the earliest days of tea drinking in France, milk was put in first to help protect the fine porcelain from cracking on contact with the tea. There's an old Irish saying that putting the milk in second is ideal if you have lost the tea strainer, because the milk pushes the leaves to the bottom of the cup.

The big issue, though, isn't whether you should put milk in first or second but whether you should add milk at all. After all, the first tea to come to the West was green tea, and the Chinese have always drunk it without milk. While black tea often goes well with milk, which needs a heavy tea to balance it, milk simply doesn't settle comfortably with the light and fragrant Chinese and Japanese green teas.

*Ecstasy is a glass full of tea and a piece of sugar in the mouth.*
—Aleksandr Pushkin

# To Sugar or Not to Sugar?

Tea tastes bitter, and you may take your tea with a spoonful of sugar (or a slice of lemon) to offset this taste. Sugar is optional, but when included it should always be added after the tea and before the milk (if any). If you find undissolved sugar at the bottom of the cup or mug after drinking, then you are either using too much sugar or not stirring hard enough.

After adding sugar and/or milk, stir the tea with a teaspoon. The stirring can be done in either a clockwise or counterclockwise direction, but not both as they would cancel each other out. Speed of stirring isn't critical. The production of a vortex about one-third the depth of the cup or mug will do.

If you do use sugar in addition to milk, it's best to stir the tea before as well as after adding the milk. This makes the sugar dissolve quicker and has the added bonus that if you get disturbed during the ceremony, return later, and can't remember whether you've added the sugar or not, then all you have to do is examine the surface of the tea—if it's moving in a circle, then you know you've added and stirred the sugar.

*It was as if we were at the heart of a maze. We were overwhelmed by the enormity of the tasks ahead. Mary had given us a bottle of milk and a spoonful of loose tea, and so, unable to decide what to do, we did what all Irish men and women do: we had tea. Suddenly the sun appeared and not for the first or last time we felt it uplifting us and changing everything. It seemed like a holiday.*

—Niall Williams and Christine Breen, *O Come Ye Back to Ireland*

# Nourishing Blend № 2

## *boiling is not always best*

*About Tea*: The correct water temperature is imperative for great tea. Boiling isn't always best.

*About Life*: Don't boil away with stress. Put away your to-do list at some time every day.

Most tea drinkers know that to make a great cup of tea you need to bring your water to a boil. So why is boiling not always good? The fresh boiling water rule is important, but since tea is produced in three distinct ways—black, green, and oolong—each of these styles has different water needs. If you are using black tea, then, yes, water should be boiling before it is poured, but for oolong tea it should be slightly cooler (190°F–210°F), and for green tea the water should be cooler still (180°F). If green or oolong tea is overheated, its taste is ruined, so the correct water temperature is crucial when making and serving a great tea.

It's the same in life. Do you sometimes feel as if you haven't got the temperature right and you're boiling over with stress?

# Black, Green, or Oolong?
# It's a Matter of Processing

The drinking of tea can be a marvelous vehicle for armchair travel. Cup in hand, you can explore Cameroon, Malawi, the mountains of Nuwara Eliya in Sri Lanka, the Nilgiri hills in the south of India, or China's seventeen tea-growing provinces and their plantations. Although it is possible to make black, green, or oolong from any tea plant in any tea region, the type of tea that is produced from freshly plucked leaves is driven mainly by geography and by tradition. India and Sri Lanka, for example, tend to produce black tea, Taiwan favors oolong, and Japan produces green tea.

It's the processing, however, that decides what type of tea is produced, with variations in the procedure determining whether a tea is black, green, oolong, or a variation such as a blended or flavored tea. As you might expect, green tea is the least processed of all the tea types.

For black tea, the plump, moist, and freshly picked leaves are spread out on vast trays in an airy, shaded area for up to twenty-four hours to wither. As the moisture evaporates, the leaves shrivel until they are ready for the next stage, rolling, where they are rolled and twisted lengthwise by huge rotary machines or, in the case of fine teas, rolled by hand. Rolling starts the process of oxidation, known as fermentation, when the leaf turns a coppery, autumnal color. It's during fermentation that the classic characteristics of the individual teas develop, and generally the longer the fermentation, the deeper the flavor. To stop the fermentation, the leaves are fired—heated to dry them and give them their distinctive color. The processes of withering, fermentation, and firing take great skill; since the moisture content of the leaves varies daily, under- or overestimating any one of these stages can spoil the tea. Finally, the teas are graded and packed in foil-lined wooden boxes ready for transport. Some of the best-known black teas come from India, Sri Lanka, and China.

Green teas were the first teas to be enjoyed in the world, but they have been overtaken in popularity by black tea. Perhaps the stresses of daily life required a stronger tea, or the elegance of the drink without milk or sugar is too subtle for Western tastes. Certainly green tea is an acquired taste, and the tea can develop a distinctive, bitter flavor if made too strong. Green tea is a brilliant digestive aid, though, and the health benefits are beginning to be recognized by Western medical research. It's high in vitamins C and B and fluoride, and research suggests it may be helpful in preventing heart disease and cancer. In making green tea, the leaves are neither fermented nor withered. The freshly picked leaves are simply rolled and then dried quickly to stop them from going brown. The leaves are then sorted and graded. Typically, green teas are produced in China and Japan.

*Oolong* means "black dragon" in Chinese. It's a term used to describe tea that is semifermented; that is, the leaves are fermented and withered very briefly. The leaves are shaken during fermentation and then fired to the point that the leaves develop peachy notes. Some of the best oolongs come from Taiwan. Flower names are used for quality teas—peony, white rose, and peach blossom. Oolongs should be drunk Chinese style in a bowl and topped up with boiling water when necessary. A rare specialty is monkey-picked oolong, which has a heavenly fragrance and an exotic flavor. Traditionally monkeys were used to gather wild leaves that had seeded themselves in crevices and on steep cliffs, and only a few pounds of this tea appear on the market at any one time.

*Tea does our fancy aid, repress those vapours which the head invade and keeps the palace of the soul serene.*
—Edmund Waller (1606–1687), British poet

*Great love affairs start with champagne and end with tisane.*
—Honore de Balzac

# Variations on a Theme

Blended teas such as English breakfast tea were invented a century ago using black Indian and China teas to create a strong brew to drink with milk. Today's English breakfast tea also contains Assam tea for strength, Ceylon tea for flavor, and African tea for color. The United Kingdom has other regional blends, such as Yorkshire tea and Irish breakfast tea. The Irish are devoted to tea drinking and once declared that the best tea went to China and the next best to Ireland.

Flavored teas go back centuries: the Chinese added flowers, and the Indians and Arabs added spices, such as rose and jasmine, to enhanced flavor. Today you can find teas with an exotic range of natural flavorings, from peach to apple crumble to sticky toffee.

Perhaps the most famous flavored tea is Earl Grey, which was the first flavored tea in the West. A blend of Indian and China teas flavored with the oil of bergmot, a small citrus fruit, the tea was named after Earl Grey (1764–1845), who was prime minister under William IV. Jasmine is another delicious flavored tea. Green tea is scented with jasmine flowers, picked in the morning when the blossoms are closed and added to tea in the afternoon when they are about to open.

Herbal teas, or *tisanes,* are highly regarded for their medical benefits—for easing an unsettled stomach or calming anxiety or simply as a caffeine-free alternative. Classic varieties include chamomile, peppermint, and lemon balm, but there are a whole range of colorful varieties containing fruit and flowers as well as herbs and spices. Tisanes do not last as well as tea, and for best results, buy little and often.

# Boiling Point!

Time is running out. The traffic has slowed right down, and you're running late. Your mind goes over all the to-do's on your list today, but the traffic isn't moving faster, the kids start arguing in the back of the car, you can hear your cell phone ringing in your bag, and you start to panic. Your heart beats faster, your temper rises, your stomach churns, and you feel a headache coming on. Welcome to the world of stress.

We all know what it feels like when life's demands seem to get the best of us. Everyone experiences stress, whether working in a demanding or repetitive job, looking after a home and family, or juggling the two. Stress is a natural part of modern life.

When we face a threatening situation, the brain puts the body on alert by producing more of the so-called fight-or-flight hormones, adrenaline and noradrenaline. These can raise blood pressure, increase heart rate, restrict blood flow to the skin, reduce stomach activity, causing a feeling of butterflies, and increase perspiration. At the same time the body also produces cortisol, which can release sugar and fat into the system and reduce the efficiency of the immune system, so we fight infections less well.

These physical changes are useful if we are at risk in some way, as they prepare the organs and muscles we need in an emergency, like the heart and legs, and divert supplies from those we don't, like the digestive system. This gives us extra energy to think and move fast. If you were running from an attacker, you would need this energy!

But the body reacts in this same way when you are stuck in a supermarket line or overwhelmed with to-do's, and if you have no chance to use up the adrenaline produced, you'll feel even more wound up.

# Iced Tea

Tea merchant Richard Blechynden brought his tea to the 1904 World's Fair in St. Louis, but nobody wanted to taste his hot tea because there was a heat wave. In desperation, he put ice in his brewed tea, and it was an instant hit. Today Americans consume more iced tea than hot.

Perhaps the biggest reason iced tea is such a booming success in the United States is that it's so convenient and easy. Food service operators just need an iced-tea brewer; the tea fits nicely into a bottle, can, or container; and there is no limit to the flavors you can find on ice: vanilla, bergamot, ginger, and grapefruit, to name a few. It's also easy to make a great cup of iced tea at home.

To make the perfect cup of iced tea, measure 4 teaspoons of strong Ceylon tea or a delicate Darjeeling into a 6-cup pot and cover with cold water. Avoid brewing with boiling water like regular tea, as this brings out too much tannin and the tea can go cloudy when cool. Chill for 5 hours, then strain and serve, sweetening to taste. Serve in tall glasses with ice cubes and lemon slices and mint sprigs for garnish.

The way we react to stress today is the same way we've reacted for thousands of years when survival was at stake and at any moment we could have been attacked or eaten. However, in modern life there is no logical need for this response, and in most situations, like waiting at an airport or when the children are shouting, we get ourselves unnecessarily worked up. And if the body stays on red alert for a long time—boosting some parts at the expense of others—it can affect our physical and mental health. Recently, scientists have learned more about how prolonged stress can affect us. The same chemical reactions that cause short-term symptoms can create longer-term health problems.

Studies have shown that an inefficient immune system can make you more prone to flu and other viruses. Permanently raised blood pressure can increase your risk of a heart attack or stroke. Too much fat in the blood can clog the arteries, which also increases your risk of heart disease. Some studies even suggest stress may be a risk factor for depression, hormonal problems, infertility, cancer, and poor health in general.

It's not all bad news, though. Just as black tea needs water that has reached boiling point, some pressure can be good for us. Challenging yourself or trying out new things makes life stimulating and exciting. Too little stress and life gets very dull. A moderate amount of stress can push you in a positive direction, forcing you to make changes and move forward with your life. Studies have shown that students perform badly in exams when they are under too little stress, just as when they have too much stress. They succeed best with a medium amount of stress. You can apply that to other things in life. Too little stress and you'll feel bored and unchallenged, but too much stress and your health, work performance, and relationships will suffer.

*Tea is drunk to forget the din of the world.*
—T'ien Yiheng, eighth-century Chinese sage

## Why Do We Get Ourselves Worked Up?

We know we are not normally facing life-threatening dangers when we feel stressed. So why do we act as if we are still being chased by a saber-toothed tiger?

Some experts believe feeling stressed is a modern problem brought on by the ever-increasing pace of life. They argue that outside pressures, like changing work practices, the fast pace of life, and a modern culture that worships success and money—wanting a bigger house, bigger TV, and bigger car—at the expense of just being a good person are mainly to blame. Others believe life is no more stressful now than it has ever been. They say stress is largely a creation of our own minds. Some people seem to thrive on a hectic lifestyle. Others find small demands stressful. We are all unique in the way we respond to pressure. Clearly, how much stress we experience has to do not just with what happens to us but also with the way we think about and cope with pressure.

## Recognize the Warning Signs

Learning to recognize the warning signs so that we can take action to help us cope better is one of the key steps to weathering the storm.

We all react differently under stress, and the initial health effects can vary, but typically physical symptoms include headaches, stomach upsets, feeling sick, aches and pains, shaking, sweating, insomnia, and increased colds and infections. Mental changes include feelings of panic or anxiety, irritability, depression, poor concentration, feeling helpless, lacking confidence, and withdrawing from loved ones and friends.

Most people experience these sorts of problems at stressful times in their lives. Nobody should feel embarrassed or guilty because their body is telling them to slow down or take a break. Usually these symptoms are not indications of anything serious and will go away when the stressful situation disappears. But they are signs that you should recognize you are under stress, and action should be taken to remove the stress or find better ways of dealing with it.

## Keeping Your Cool

Losing your cool? Can't cope? Feeling stressed? Here are some commonsense tips to help you cope better with stress. Remember, they are not fixed in stone. Giving yourself more to-do's—on top of life's existing demands—will only make matters worse. Just pick and choose the ideas you find helpful.

### 1. Look after yourself

To avoid burnout, decide to eat well—remember you are what you eat—and exercise regularly. All forms of exercise can help get rid of the pent-up feeling that stress creates and release hormones that promote a sense of well-being. Exercise gives your mind and body a positive challenge. Try to get into a regular routine of exercising for at least 30 minutes three times a week. Many people find rhythmic exercise—swimming, running, or cycling—is particularly good for overcoming stress.

## 2. Forget about being perfect

You don't need to be perfect. It is okay to do work that is good enough. Perfectionists are often the first victims of stress. You don't have to excel all the time. When you take on a task, check what is expected. There is no point in writing a twenty-four-page report when all that is needed is a brief memo. And if you make a mistake or forget to do something important or don't get what you want or just mess up, remember, we all make mistakes. Write it off to experience. It does not mean you personally are a failure.

## 3. It's okay to say no

Don't take on more than you can handle. Be assertive. It is okay to say no to other people's demands. You just need the right technique. Try saying, "Yes, I can do this report, but it will mean I cannot make that meeting." Or simply say, "Thank you for asking me, but I am afraid I would not be able to meet that deadline." Let people know how busy you are. You can put a red card on your computer when you don't want to be interrupted, a green one when that's okay. The same applies for friends and family. If you have too much on your plate and can't run an errand or do a favor, tell them that you'd love to help out but this time you can't. It's important for them to understand that you have a life of your own too. It's important that you understand that relationships are about give-and-take, and it really is okay for you to say no from time to time.

## 4. Take action if you can

Sometimes worrying about what to do in a situation can be more stressful than actually doing it, so if you can take action and create positive change, do it. You need to weigh the pros and cons and think carefully about the course of action you take, but sometimes we all need to feel the fear and do it anyway. These changes may be small ones, such as rearranging your work schedule or delegating tasks, or they may be big ones, such as handing in your notice or ending a relationship. Remember, long-term stress can be dangerous, and not taking action may have far worse consequences than doing something, however small. Don't beat yourself up if the action you take doesn't work out perfectly. Instead, learn from it.

But what if you feel you can't take any action? What if you find yourself in a situation in which you feel overwhelmed and can't see a way out? If this is the case, and if you can't find better ways to accept or cope with the situation, it's vital that you ask for help and support from friends and family or, if need be, counselors and doctors.

## 5. Express yourself

Express yourself. It's good to talk. Communicating with others—colleagues, friends, and family—is a great way to beat stress, whether you are pouring out your worries or just passing the time of day. When you have a particular problem, don't be afraid to seek help from others. If colleagues, friends, or family can't help, try helplines, where they exist. Discussing your concerns with an empathetic friend or with a competent professional helps get emotions out and provides you with emotional support. Verbalizing a problem with a person often helps you get a more objective view of your feelings and thoughts and helps you to see solutions more easily.

## 6. Work smarter, not longer

Staying healthy means keeping life in balance. Working long hours—whether that means staying late in the office or putting in extra time—is bad for your health, your performance, and your family. We all need time to unwind, to be with family and friends, to have space for ourselves and to enjoy hobbies or sports that have nothing to do with work. You need to find ways to work smarter, not longer. Delegate tasks where you can, prioritize, and practice the time management techniques in Nourishing Blend #6.

It is easy to feel under pressure to take work home just because everyone else does. The culture expects it. Break the mold. We all need boundaries between work and the rest of life to keep sane. Smarter organizations are now discouraging staff from working beyond reasonable limits. Remember the motto: Work to live, don't live to work.

## 7. Take time out

Put away your to-do list at some point each day. In today's hectic world, everyone needs to take a few moments for quiet reflection. We all have different ways of working. Some people love to live life in the fast lane. But most of us cannot work at breakneck pace every hour of the day. If we do, our performance suffers. Build in time to unwind and reflect and relax every day.

Allow for break times. When you are involved in work, study, or any other type of activity, structure some break times in your plan. A break from an activity can provide some refreshing results. Nourishing breaks can last a few minutes or for a few hours. Some break times include body stretching, a brief glance at your surroundings, a snack, or changing to another activity. Rather than doing what we call resting, taking a break time means that after we have engaged in vigorous and unrelated activity, usually we are more relaxed, refreshed, and prepared to return to a particular task.

Having time by yourself and for yourself can be very helpful in managing tension. Use that time for reflection, for single-person activity, or for just "doing nothing." In other words, at various times, get in touch with your "you." Experience who you are by thinking, feeling, and being "you" in alone time.

Taking a few minutes out to relax and be alone during a busy day is important. Breathing properly is a great way to do it. You can practice deep-breathing exercises from yoga or meditation. Or try this simple exercise: Sit quietly, shut your eyes, and allow your attention to follow your breath. Let stressful thoughts float away. Breathe in for three seconds, then out for nine. Repeat for a minute or two.

You don't have to chant or take up transcendental meditation to meditate. Much meditation involves deep, calm breathing to start the process and then concentrating on a particular object. This can be a repeated word, the ticking of a clock, or even a point in the room. Many people prefer to meditate with their eyes shut, emptying their mind of all distractions. Others use visualization techniques, imagining themselves to be in surroundings that are calm and lovely. For more tips on meditation techniques, turn to Nourishing Blend #9.

## 8. Vary your routine

On occasion, varying our usual daily procedures stimulates and refreshes us just as much as taking time out. For example, in the morning get out of bed on the other side. Shower first and brush hair and teeth later. When leaving your residence, go to class or to your office by a different route. For lunch or dinner, try a different place. Try something you have not done before. Vary your routine; stay out of the habit rut.

## 9. Have a nice cup of tea

And last, but by no means least—and you must have known this was coming—could there be any better way to relax, take time out, and de-stress than with a steaming cup of freshly brewed tea? Like music, tea can refresh the spirit and soothe a troubled mind at any time of the day.

# Black Tea Varieties

## India

**Assam:** Assam's teas are grown in the fertile rolling hills of the Brahmaputra River, and most of them are rich and strong with small leaves—ideally suited for breakfast and small blends.

**Darjeeling:** The altitude, cool air, and clean environment of the tea estates in the foothills of the Himalayas make for outstanding teas. Because of their altitude, Darjeeling tea bushes have a very distinct season, and the higher up they are grown, the lighter the tea. The first flush, picked in April, is light and fragrant and a special treat for tea connoisseurs. Darjeeling is known as the champagne of teas and shouldn't really be swamped with milk—unless the tea is of a lower grade. Like champagne, it is expensive, so expect to pay top prices for top-grade, named-estate Darjeelings.

**Nilgiri:** This black tea comes from the southern tip of India. Lighter than Assam tea, it has a bright, clean, and fresh taste.

## Sri Lanka

**Ceylon:** The hilly region in the southwest of this semitropical island has ideal conditions for producing wonderful tea with remarkably different styles and tastes. Some of the best teas come from the Uva district, which produces pale-colored, slightly astringent teas.

## China

**Keemun:** This is China's most famous black tea, and it comes from the Anhwei Province. It was one of the first teas developed by the Chinese for export and has a smooth, slightly sweet taste. China has a number of other black teas, most notably Yunnan and Szechuan, but none are as robust as Keemun.

**Lapsang souchong:** This is the tea with the famous smoky aroma. Not as popular as it once was for drinking, it may be coming into its own in cooking: some chefs are beginning to experiment with it as a flavoring for foods such as custard and ice cream. Never make Lapsang tea too strong; just a pinch in the pot will do.

*continued*

### Africa

The best African teas come from Kenya, Rwanda, Burundi, and Zimbabwe. Their small-leaf tea is particularly full-bodied and rich with a strong flavor and is often mistaken for coffee.

### South America

As in Indonesia and Sumatra, the best sites in South America are usually given over to coffee, but fairly standard tea-bag tea is produced in Argentina and Brazil.

### Georgia and Turkey

Pleasant, light teas are produced that are more like a strong Keemun than an Assam.

# Pu-erh Tea

Yunnan is a famous tea-growing province of China. It produces green, black, and oolong teas and a unique tea known as Pu-erh, which is currently enjoying great popularity. Pu-erh tea is processed through special fermentation by using green tea of the Yunnan large-leaf tea. It is thought that this tea has medicinal properties, and research verifies this claim. Pu-erh tea processing is a long-kept secret known only to a few Chinese tea masters, but it is fermented twice (just like some of the fine wines) and aged. This process is thought to bring out medicinal properties in this tea.

Pu-erh tea is not as strong as black tea and is black, brown, or red in color. It gives a sweet taste in the mouth after drinking. Pu-erh tea can be kept for a long time. In fact, the longer it is stored, the better it tastes and the higher its quality becomes. It tastes best if brewed with spring water.

# Green Tea Varieties

## China

**Gunpowder:** A mass of gray-colored, tightly rolled balls, the aptly named gunpowder tea produces a pale yellow-green liquid that has a refreshingly dry and astringent taste. Brew it lightly with just a few leaves, or it will have a bitter taste.

**White tip or silver needle:** This is tea made of the finest silvery tips of the branches that are picked for a few days at the start of the season. The tea is not fermented or rolled but is steamed dry. The pale yellowish liquid from these unopened tips is very mild and smooth with a delicate sweet taste. One of the most famous white-tip teas was picked for the emperor alone from specially cultivated bushes, and only virgins were allowed to do the picking.

## Japan

**Matcha:** This is powdered green tea that is used in the Japanese tea ceremony. It is brewed in very elaborate ceremony and is whisked to produce a frothy, astringent, vitamin C–rich drink.

**Sencha:** This is the most popular Japanese tea and perhaps the purest of all green teas. The leaves are rolled and steamed dry immediately after picking. Again, this tea should not be brewed too strong.

Tea has a soothing and energizing effect. It's an ideal stressbuster because it can calm you down but also provide an energy boost so you don't end up nodding off or losing the plot. It's the caffeine in tea that gives you the energy boost and fosters alertness. Caffeine is a stimulant that has had a lot of bad press, but research shows that in moderation caffeine isn't the bad guy it's often made out to be. Research suggests that a moderate caffeine intake (say, two or three lightly brewed cups a day) can boost mental function and may even be linked to a decreased risk of mental decay as we age.

# Which Tea Shall I Choose?

**Breakfast:** Try a refreshing Ceylon or English breakfast tea with milk
**After lunch:** Mango, peach
**An afternoon reviver:** Earl Grey, Darjeeling, Pu-erh
**Ideal with fruitcake:** Assam, vanilla
**Bedtime soother:** Darjeeling, light China, Pu-erh

# What Is a Fine Tea?

1. A tea that is what it claims to be, with a taste and aroma that matches its name. For example, first-flush Darjeeling is a tea harvested at first flush from a recognized garden in the Darjeeling district of southern India. Blackberry tea is a tea with the aroma of fresh blackberries.
2. A tea with credentials. For example, if it is a blend of herbal and black tea, the producer will list the black tea that is used and name the herbal component; if it is flavored, the manufacturer will tell you what type of oil is used.
3. A tea that meets your criteria of perfection; it tastes great to you.

# Caffeine

Tea contains caffeine, which accounts for its refreshing, pick-me-up quality. Many people have concerns about the caffeine content in tea, as too much caffeine is unhealthy and can crank up your stress levels even more. So how much caffeine does a cup of tea contain? The answer is complicated, and much depends on the type of tea you are drinking—for example, black tea tends to have a higher caffeine content than green tea—and the method of brewing used; longer steeping time will extract more caffeine. Bearing in mind that methods of brewing can affect caffeine content, you might find useful the following U.S. Food and Drug Administration estimate of caffeine content in 6 ounces of tea.

Black: 25–110 mg

Green: 8–36 mg

Oolong: 12–55 mg

Commercially brewed: 20–80 mg

Generally, tea contains far less caffeine than coffee: black tea usually contains about half the caffeine of coffee, green tea only one-sixth to one-eighth as much. The amount in any given cup varies with brewing methods of steeping. Tea bags tend to produce a cup with more caffeine; quickly brewed loose tea has less.

If you want tea without the kick, decaffeinated tea is available as leaves or tea bags. The caffeine is removed using substances that remove caffeine easily and effectively. The only drawback is that decaffeination can bring changes to the flavor of the tea, giving it a fruity or sweet taste. To avoid this, there is a simple method for partially decaffeinating that you can do at home. Because caffeine is so easily dissolved in water, much of the caffeine present in a cup of tea produced by traditional steeping methods will be dissolved in the first minute or so. You can take advantage of this to lower your caffeine content with a minimal loss of flavor and aroma by doing the following:

- Place a tea bag in your cup or mug, or measure tea as you normally do in your pot.
- Pour the hot water over the tea, and set your timer for a minute.
- When the minute is up, pour off the liquid and discard.
- Heat fresh water to the right temperature for the tea you want to drink, pour it over the wet leaves, and allow to steep for the usual 3 to 5 minutes.

For a naturally caffeine-free infusion, a tisane is ideal; peppermint and chamomile are particularly soothing. We take a closer look at the remarkable healing and restoring benefits of tea and herbal teas later, but for now why not take time out to de-stress and celebrate glorious simplicity with a nice cup of soothing and refreshing tea?

# Nourishing Blend № 3
## *know what's in the water*

**About Tea:** A cup of tea is a small amount of tea and a whole lot of water. Knowing what's in the water you use is critical to producing great tea.

**About Life:** Getting to know yourself better is critical for success and happiness in life. Become aware of your unique talents and potentials, and find ways to develop them.

Just as you need to know what's in the water you use in your tea, you need to get to know yourself better and find out what kind of person you are. As you read this chapter you'll discover that you are not always the person that you think you are, and when the real you stands up you may get a surprise!

## Get to Know Yourself

Just as water is tea's main ingredient, understanding yourself is the vital ingredient for a happy life. How well do you know yourself? What kind of person are you? What is important to you? Are you doing what you want to do with your life? Why do you think and feel the way you do? How happy are you with your life?

Don't worry if you don't know the answers to any of these questions. The important thing right now is that you start asking them, because each time you pause and reflect about who you are, why you do the things you do, and why you feel the way you do, you will be getting to know yourself a bit better.

Self-knowledge is the beginning of wisdom. You don't need to go overboard, though; your aim is to become more aware of why you do things so that you can make positive changes in your life, not so you will become self-obsessed. Dip in and out of the exercises in this chapter, and remember the principle of balance outlined in Nourishing Blend #1 so that you always balance me-time with time for others.

It might help to act as an observer of your own life. Step outside yourself, and take a look at what you think, feel, say, and do. You've never tried it? Then you don't know how easy it is; it's a well-known technique for improving self-awareness. Stepping back and watching yourself can help you separate what you think and feel from who you are. You will see that throughout the day thoughts and feelings are constantly flow through you. You will see that as powerful as these feelings and thoughts are, they are separate from you. You are the one who allows yourself to experience them. You are the one in charge.

If you want to feel fulfilled and happy, self-awareness is key. You need to look at the way you live your life, the way you think, and the way you feel. As you start to get to know yourself, you will start to recognize patterns of behavior—responses or attitudes—that make you unhappy, and only when you start to recognize what makes you unhappy can you start making positive changes. And the first of these positive changes needs to be your self-image.

*Come along inside. . . . We'll see if tea and buns can make the world a better place.*
—Kenneth Grahame, *The Wind in the Willows*

# Know Your Water

To make great-tasting tea you need good-quality water. Historically, tea-houses in China and the United States were located next to wells, and it was common knowledge that the water from these special places was what made the tea outstanding. Today you can still find water prejudice; many Chinese still insist that spring water makes the best cup, and in the States, Seattle water is thought it be among the best for brewing tea. But what if you don't live near a freshwater spring? What should you look for?

Well, there should be no tastes or aromas in the water to mask the taste of your tea. If your water is earthy or highly chlorinated, you could use filtered or bottled water when you are brewing. Other factors also affect the taste of the water, such as calcium and oxygen levels, and to avoid a flat, lifeless cup of tea, you should always fill your kettle with freshly drawn water and not water that has been sitting for hours in a kettle or boiler. The bottom line is the water you use should be fresh, clean, odorless, refreshing, and something you'd be happy to drink. If you wouldn't drink it out of your tap or bottle, don't use it to make your tea.

## Do You Like What You See?

You can use anything about yourself as a starting point for self-awareness. Take your favorite tea, for example. Has it become a habit? Do you think it might say something about the kind of person you are? Find the tea that you drink the most often, and then go to the personality trait list in "Your Cup of Tea?" on page 54 and see what it might say about you.

# Your Cup of Tea?

**Black tea drinker:** You're a forward-looking, intense person. Your thoughts are always directed toward the future: "How can I do this differently?" You have a fertile and active mind that is always churning. The downside is that this can mean you can come across as intense and detached.

**Green tea drinker:** A connoisseur of the fine things in life, you know what you are talking about, and you are a specialist—a visionary—in your field. The downside is this can make you dictatorial in your dealings with others. People have to fit into your idea of living; otherwise, you have no time for them.

**Blended tea drinker:** You would have all the power of the universe behind you if only you knew what you wanted in life. All options are open to you, but which one will you take? It can be hard to make decisions because of all the choices you have. Always weighing the pros and cons, you can see both sides of an argument. This can cloud your thoughts, but when you make a decision you have all the force with you.

*For tea, though ridiculed by those who are naturally coarse in their nervous sensibilities, or are become so fine from wine drinking and are not susceptible of influence from so refined a stimulant, will always be the favored beverage of the intellectual.*
—Thomas De Quincy, *Confessions of an English Opium Eater*

Don't take all this too seriously. It's a fun exercise, but thinking about the things you like and don't like, even the kind of tea you drink, can get you thinking about the kind of person you are and the way you project yourself to others. Are you thoughtful? Do you

**Oolong tea drinker:** Facing the world with joy, you see the hidden potential in everyone you meet. You thrive on challenge and can achieve much in this life through hard work and discipline, but there's also a part of you that loves excitement, danger, and freedom from routine.

**Flavored tea drinker:** You like to live in the past emotionally, to love that sweet, smooth feeling that is the pure essence of childhood. You love to remember past happiness, a time when things were simple and straightforward, but by so doing you might have a tendency to neglect the present.

**Herbal tea drinker:** You're flexible and can fit into any situation, anytime, anywhere. You have an all-around knowledge of all walks of life and can move with the times. You don't like to be left behind, which means that sometimes you're so busy playing catch-up you forget to look where you are going.

**Iced tea drinker:** All things are possible to iced tea lovers; you have all the scope of life to choose from. You tend to see life as moving on; tomorrow is another day. You're very clear on what you are doing, full of ideas, and won't be bound by rules unless you made them. You're always striving for things to be better and looking ahead with excitement. The downside is that there could be problems with letting go and trusting yourself, and suffering from the past could be clouding your judgment of the here and now.

enjoy a good gossip? Are you a good friend? What impression do you give to others? Are you warm and friendly or cold and detached? Are you being true to yourself or acting a role? The really important question is this: Is the role I am choosing to create one that makes me happy?

If you want great-tasting tea, you need to know what's in the water. If you want to enjoy life, you need to take a good long look at yourself. Have you created an image that works for you? Would challenging some of your habits—even ones you think don't matter, like the way you take your tea—be a way to reinvent yourself?

## The Main Ingredient

Water is the main ingredient of tea, but it's the one that gets the least attention. Your self-esteem is the most important thing in your life, but it too rarely gets the attention it deserves. Your self-image, like the water you use for your tea, needs to be of a certain quality. If your self-esteem is good, you will attract success and happiness into your life. If it's low, you will find that happiness and success slipping through your fingers.

Your self-esteem guides you through life in much the same way that a steering wheel guides a car. Until you grab hold of the wheel and steer the car in the direction you want to go, you'll end up going nowhere or in the wrong direction. If your self-image is low, your life will be directionless. So how can you get yourself back on course and drive yourself where you want to go? You start working on the first and most important of all ingredients for happiness: self-esteem.

*Bill Bryson, Notes from a Small Island: He brewed his tea in a blue china pot, poured it into a chipped white cup with forget-me-nots on the handle, and dropped in a dollop of honey and cream. He sat by the window, cup in hand, watching the first snow fall. "I am," he sighed deeply, "contented as a clam. I am a most happy man."*
—Ethel Pochocki, *Wildflower Tea*

## Ten Ways to Boost Self-Esteem

### 1. Find your center

Start by asking yourself how much your self-esteem is centered on the job you have, the clothes you wear, the way you look, the people you know, the money you earn, the things you have. There is nothing wrong with wealth and success, but centering your life on these things will lead you astray. Self-esteem has to come from within, not from without—from the quality of your heart, not the quality of the things you own or the things you do. After all, those who die with the most money still die. An old saying conveys the message far better than I can: "If all I am is what I have and what I have is lost, then who am I?"

The only center that actually works as a basis for your self-esteem is a center built on principles. Live by your principles and you will excel; break them and you will fail or feel discontent. Here are a few examples of principles to live by: honesty, love, respect, loyalty, responsibility, and balance. There are many more, and your heart will easily recognize them. It takes faith to live by principles; it can be hard when you see others getting ahead by lying, cheating, and manipulating. To grasp why sound principles always work, imagine a life based on their opposites—hate, dishonesty, selfishness, extremes. Can you imagine any lasting happiness coming out of that?

Ironically, putting principles first is the key to boosting self-esteem and doing better in all areas of your life. For example, if you are honest and loving, you are more likely to attract loving people into your life. If you work hard, always try your best, and show respect to others, opportunities will come your way. Throughout this book you'll see that each of the nourishing blends and tea wisdom rules are based upon principles; that's where they get their power.

## 2. Tap into your talents

Finding and then developing a talent, hobby, or special interest can be one of the greatest things you can do to boost your self-esteem. Each person as a unique being has abilities and talents they can develop and use for healthy and productive living. Become aware of your unique talents and potentials.

Focus on your strengths, not your weaknesses. Talents come in a variety of packages, so expand your thinking beyond musical ability or athletic prowess. Think big, not small. Do you have a knack for speaking, dancing, writing, or drawing? Perhaps you are a fast learner, or perhaps you have the gift of being accepting of others. You may have organizational skills or leadership skills. It doesn't matter where your talent lies, whether it is in drama, train spotting, or knitting, when you do something you are good at (have a talent for), it's exhilarating. It's a form of self-expression, and it builds self-esteem.

But what if you don't know where your talents lie? If that's the case, think about what makes you feel good about yourself. If you are lacking in inspiration, take a sip of tea; it quickens the pulse and refreshes the spirit. Your creativity is just waiting to surface. What makes your heart sing? We all have talents; we just need to find out what they are. The following questions will help you focus on what truly inspires you.

- Think of a song or a book or an animal or a landscape or a film that represents you. Then think about why it represents you.
- If you could be one person for a day, who would that person be? It can be anyone alive or dead from any moment in time. Why did you choose that person? What draws you to him or her?
- If you were given one month a year to do exactly what you wanted, what would that be?
- If someone wrote your autobiography, what would the title be?

These questions are designed to get you thinking about what you want out of life and what is important to you. Without water, tea is lifeless and dry. If you don't know what you want from life, life feels meaningless. Don't expect overnight answers; many of us change direction many times and search for a lifetime to find what brings us to life. The important thing is that you begin the search and bring movement and a sense of anticipation into your life. Inspiration may be just around the corner.

## 3. Let's play pretend

One way to boost confidence about yourself is simply to pretend that you are a confident person. Pretending to be confident is just a starting point, and the more you do it, the more it will become second nature. If you feel insecure, try to appear calm even if you don't feel it. Before you enter a room, collect yourself, stand tall, and walk purposefully. Imagine you are a movie star or a politician if it helps. Act confident. Tell yourself what you are doing as if you are playing a tape in your head, as this will stop you thinking about how you are feeling. For example, "I'm walking toward the door, I've got a drink in my hand," and so on. Maintain eye contact with the people you meet, and speak clearly; believe in the words you say. Smile—it not only makes you look more confident, it also helps relax you so that you feel more confident. If nerves do bubble over, don't panic. Everyone feels nervous from time to time; it's all part of being human. A bit of nerves has its plus side too; it sharpens your performance and sends out signals that you care and want to do well.

Finally, work to change your self-image at a subconscious level by using your imagination—a technique called visualization. See yourself as confident and calm. Picture how life would be if you believed in yourself. See yourself succeeding. You may think this is just daydreaming or wishful thinking, but it's not. Visualization is a powerful technique that can help build self-esteem and boost your chances of success in life. As you start to believe in yourself more, you will start to feel more confident and strong, and when you start to feel like that, other people will see strength in you too. They will react to you differently. You'll feel better, think better, and look better and become the calm, confident person you imagined yourself to be. As you grow in confidence, you begin to change your ideas about success and happiness. You don't hope for it, you believe in and expect it.

## 4. Take up the challenge

If you meet up with obstacles and setbacks, try to think of them as challenges, not problems. This is such a powerful self-help tool that we'll explore it in more detail later, but for now tell yourself that you are a creative and resourceful person and you can rise above whatever obstacles life puts in your path. The Chinese symbol for crisis is also the symbol for opportunity. What a great way to think about an obstacle! Instead of being a problem, it becomes a challenge to your inventiveness. Take up the challenge, and see it as an opportunity for you to learn, grow, and take control of your life.

## 5. Stay away from grumpy people

Do you know someone who is always complaining? Do you enjoy spending time with them? Probably not! If there are people in your life who make you feel low, stay away from them, even if they are close friends or family members. They are determined that they and you will never have a good day. They are victims of life and want to stay that way—but you don't.

Feeling good about the people you mix with is an important indicator of happiness. Who do you enjoy being with? Who lifts you up? Who would you like to share a cup of tea with? If life gets tough, who would you turn to for support, people who told you that you couldn't do something or people who told you to believe in yourself?

Steer clear of people who drag you down. Like attracts like: happiness attracts happiness, and negativity attracts negativity. Mix with people who make you feel good about yourself and your life.

Positive relationships with other people help to build self-esteem. True self-worth can only come from within, but at times we all need to feel listened to, supported, and reassured by others. Reassurance is the feeling that things will be all right in the end. In today's fragmented, fast-moving world it can be hard to retain a sense of connection; isolation and loneliness are modern epidemics. So how do you go about regaining a sense of connection to others? Start by spending more time with family, friends, and loved ones. Schedule time together. Play more. Talk more. Don't neglect your colleagues, either, and the ties you have with neighbors. Nurture positive connections with the people in your life. You may find solace and a sense of connection by turning to prayer or meditation. Talking to God or, if you are not religious, to a higher source might help you feel connected to the world, to nature, to time, to space. Cultivating a network of support can be the most healing thing you ever do for yourself.

Don't forget, though, that although we find meaning through our relationships with others, how we feel about ourselves is just as significant. We need to feel loved and supported by others, but we also need to be able to love and support ourselves. True contentment is possible only if we meet all our love needs, both the love we give to others and the love we give to ourselves. Other people can lift your mood and support and value you, but ultimately your health and well-being reside with you. If you saw your best friend neglecting their health, I'm sure you would be concerned and would encourage a change in attitude. Do the same for yourself. You are the best friend you will ever have. Take care of yourself.

## 6. Enjoy yourself

Having fun is one of the best and most neglected ways to feel better about yourself. Many studies have linked happiness to good health and long life. The positive emotions associated with laughter decrease stress hormones and increase the number of immune cells. So the more fun you have, the more gracefully you will age and the healthier you will feel. Many of us take ourselves far too seriously. Having fun and playing needn't stop when you're no longer a child. Think about all the things you really enjoy doing, and then try to work as many of them as possible into your daily life. After all, if you don't have enjoyment, fun, and laughter in your life, are you really living?

One of the biggest stumbling blocks to enjoying life is a poor self-image. Feeling unattractive stops many of us from living life to the full. Body image insecurity affects every aspect or our lives and is a major cause of anxiety and low self-esteem. Changing your diet, your exercise routine, your wardrobe, or your hairstyle can give a temporary boost to body image, but for that boost to become permanent you have to start trying to change the way you think about yourself. This won't be easy, and you need to be patient with yourself, as you'll be fighting years of negative conditioning. Here are some tips that might help:

- Being thin and beautiful does not equal happiness or high self-esteem. Behind the glossy pictures of celebrities gracing magazine covers, you'll often find insecurity and unhappiness.
- Think about the people you consider beautiful. Often their features or their bodies are not perfect. Recognize that it is unnatural and unhealthy to look like models on the catwalk and that many celebrity photos are airbrushed. These are not real people but fantasies created by the media and the public's wishes for perfection.
- Get to know your body better. Look at yourself in the mirror, and counteract negative thoughts with positive ones. Instead of thinking, "I look fat," focus on how beautiful your eyes are or how good your hair looks or how great you look in a certain color.
- Focus on what you are good at. Put your energy into things you enjoy. Feeling fulfilled makes a person attractive at whatever age or weight.

- Treat your body well, and give it healthy food and regular exercise. Body confidence begins when you start to treat your body with respect.
- Rethink your definition of attractiveness. Beauty is not about youth and slenderness but about feeling confident about yourself and happy with your life. The sooner you come to this realization, the happier and more beautiful you will be.

## 7. Improve your communication skills

If you can't communicate well with others, self-esteem is likely to remain fragile. You won't be able to get your point of view across or your needs met, and this can make you feel inadequate. Talking is a natural skill, but effective communication needs to be learned. The following suggestions may help:

- Learn to listen. Allow other people to express their thoughts and feelings without constantly interrupting with your own. Really listen to what others are saying, and don't think about what your response will be. Don't always feel the need to advise or criticize; just restate or reflect back what the other person has said to you to show that you have been listening.
- Communication is a two-way process, and as well as listening to someone else, you also want to be listened to, but wait until the other person is ready to listen. And after you've had your say, there's nothing wrong with asking if they understood what you said.
- Don't be afraid of silence in conversations. In times of silence you can collect your thoughts. A great deal can be said in times of silence: I'm listening, I'm understanding, I'm there for you.
- Stay objective, and avoid blaming others for the way you feel. Instead of blaming another, focus attention on the consequence.

For instance, say, "*This* made me feel anxious," instead of "*You* are making me anxious."

- Use questions that facilitate communication, such as, "How do you feel about that?" or "What happened?" Avoid any questions that are interrogating.
- Say what you mean without causing offense. In other words, be diplomatic. For example, don't tell someone you don't like what that person is wearing; say you think another style or color might flatter them better.
- Remember, the only person who has the right to judge your behavior and actions is you, and you have the right at any time to say no, to change your mind, to say, "I don't understand," "I don't know," or even "I don't care." The more you start being honest and saying what you really want—and saying no if need be—the more your communication skills and your self-esteem will improve.

## 8. Celebrate your uniqueness

How often do you compare yourself to other people? Do you ever feel you just aren't as good as or as clever as or as beautiful as someone else? Every time you compare yourself with someone else, you are mistrusting yourself.

Comparing yourself to others is a sure route to low self-esteem. There will always be people who are better than you in some things. That's just a fact of life. The success of other people doesn't matter; what matters is how successful you feel you are. Other people don't have the same background, skills, personality, and challenges you have. Your life journey will never be the same as anyone else's. Concentrate on your own life, your skills, your talents, and what makes you unique.

Whenever you feel the urge to compare yourself negatively or fit in, look carefully at whatever it is that makes you different. Accept and make the most of these features; your differences are what make you an original. You are unique. There isn't going to be another person like you on this planet ever again. Doesn't that make you feel special? Remind yourself of how unique you are. Celebrate that uniqueness.

Notice when you start to think negatively about yourself, and replace those thoughts with more positive ones about yourself. For example, every time you think, "I'm a loser," replace that with something positive like, "I am a winner." Repetition is important here, and it may take a few weeks before you notice an improvement. Simply keep trying. You are throwing out the old and sending new data to your subconscious mind, and these new thoughts will eventually become the foundation stone of your success.

As you practice these new skills, self-confidence will gradually replace the need for the approval of others. You begin to understand that the most important thing is whether or not you are being true to yourself. You don't need others to validate your every action and thought. You begin to trust your own opinions. You start being yourself. Only when you are yourself and you are happy to be yourself will self-esteem finally be yours. The quickest way to improve your self-esteem is to be yourself. Expect this to feel scary at first. But in time, having the courage to be yourself and think your own thoughts is one of the most truly wonderful gifts you can give yourself. You'll start to see that the quality of your life doesn't depend on what other people think or on what happens to you but on how you choose to react to it. We'll explore the power of choice, but for now just bear in mind that nobody can make you doubt yourself or your abilities without your consent. The choice is always yours. You can choose to doubt yourself, or you can choose to live your life on your own terms.

## 9. Enjoy your aloneness

Find a place to be alone and enjoy your own company. Allow your thoughts to run wild. Rediscover dreams and possibilities. Enjoy yourself. Some of us find it harder to be alone than others. But you are the only person who ever truly knows you. No one else can be you. You can see this aloneness as isolating, or you can see it as a wonderful kind of freedom. How you live is truly up to you.

And finally, when you have the courage to be yourself and to enjoy yourself, you will also find that you have the courage to let go.

## 10. Let go

Letting go doesn't mean not caring; it means not taking responsibility for what other people do, feel, or think. It means allowing others to choose their own decisions and learn from their mistakes. It means accepting that you are not all-powerful and can't always determine the outcome of events. It means not trying to change or blame others and making the most of yourself without putting others down. It means having the courage to look at your own shortcomings. It means striving to be true to yourself and helping others to be true to themselves. It means looking at the larger picture instead of being preoccupied with the details.

It's impossible to be in control of every detail of your life. Sometimes you just have to take a risk and let go. You may make a decision or change your mind about something. Is this the best thing? You may never know, but at least you are seeking a solution and your life is moving forward.

Life finds its meaning when you face your fears instead of avoiding them. You can't always know if you are doing the right thing, but every time you search for an answer, you are adding to your store of knowledge and life experience. Instead of letting low self-esteem and self-doubt put your life on hold, do what you were put on this Earth to do: live, learn, and grow.

## A Lifetime's Work and Joy

On a bad day, when self-image or self-esteem is low and spiraling downward to the pit of negativity, you see a world in which everyone seems cleverer, happier, richer, more successful, and better able to cope than you. Of course, everyone else isn't like this; it's just the way it seems when you feel low about yourself and your life.

Everyone struggles with issues of self-esteem, even those really cool, confident-looking people. Self-esteem is always an issue. It goes up and down with amazing speed for each and every one of us. We are all working on our self-esteem and our personal development. We all need to work on our sense of self-worth. Our self-esteem is like a beautiful flower or plant: it needs constant nourishment and care in order for it to grow and thrive. You are not alone; this job is a lifetime's work and joy for all of us.

All the tips in this chapter and indeed throughout the book are designed to help you pull yourself out of negativity and increase good feelings about yourself. Don't get down if you lose your self-esteem—it happens to everyone, all the time. However, as you learn ways to bring positive changes in your life, your self-esteem will become much more stable. Next time you feel disheartened you will be able to pick yourself up, dust yourself off, reflect a while over a nice cup of tea, and start again with renewed confidence.

# Nourishing Blend № 4

## *choose the right teapot*

**About Tea:** Make sure you aren't using a teapot that you dislike, no matter how good its reputation, because as a constant daily companion it will make you feel uncomfortable.

**About Life:** You are what you believe yourself to be. Make sure that the way you think about yourself isn't destroying the quality of your life.

Develop a sound philosophy. Epictetus, a first-century AD philosopher, said, "People are disturbed not by things but the view which they take from them." Becoming aware of how your thoughts affect your feelings can be a big step forward, and once you start to recognize negative thinking patterns, you can start to replace them with other thoughts. Changing your thoughts can change your life.

## Your Best Friends and Your Worst Enemies Are Your Thoughts

The finest tea in the world can be ruined if the teapot you are using is dirty or smelly. The fact that the teapot is referred to as the "father of tea" stresses the importance of the vessel in which tea is made. People who care about tea know that their teapots are very important and need looking after, because some pots absorb water and

# Teapots

Great tea does not stop at the kettle. The teapot is just as vital. If you only drink Indian, Ceylon, or African tea, then one pot is all you need, but if you want to drink milder green Chinese teas, then you need another pot just for green tea. And if you like the highly perfumed teas and enjoy Earl Grey or Lapsang souchong, then you need yet another separate pot for them.

Just as fine wines demand glasses of different shapes for sherries, champagnes, clarets, and brandies, fine teas need their own teapots. You'll need a solid teapot for strong black tea, a China teapot for Chinese tea, and a floral design for Lapsang or Earl Grey. If you like glass teapots, they work as well as china, especially the ones that have a press system where the leaves are isolated at the bottom after brewing. As for specialty teas, they don't have to be made in teapots but can be made in cups or mugs. You may also decide to invest in a tea sock, which fits any size of teapot, and you can remove the leaves as soon as the tea is made.

accumulate an essence that affects the quality and flavor of the brew. In a similar way, your thoughts are crucial and need looking after. Negative thinking affects the way you feel and destroys the quality of your life.

> Tea. Earl Grey. Hot. And whoever this Earl Grey fellow is,
> I'd like to have a word with him.
> —Jean-Luc Picard, Star Trek: The Next Generation

If you think sad, bad, or negative thoughts, you are going to feel bad. If you're unhappy, you may not realize the relationship between your thought processes and your mood. Need convincing? Try this little exercise. Think of a time in your life when you enjoyed yourself. It might have been a holiday or a trip to the park. As you think about that time you may feel a bit happier. Now think of a time when you were sad, like at a funeral, and you will probably feel quite down.

Your thoughts can be your best friends or your worst enemies. They can lift you up, and they can pull you down. If you want to feel happier and calmer, you need to become aware of the way thoughts affect you and to start questioning negative thoughts. You may argue that this isn't realistic. You'd like to be more positive, but life is tough and chances are things won't work out the way you want. You're right. It is unrealistic to expect positive outcomes to everything; when you do, you set yourself up for disappointment. But the next time you are negative about something or tell yourself that you are useless or you can't cope, ask yourself instead, "Am I being realistic? Are my thoughts misleading me? Am I taking into account other possibilities?"

Don't believe everything you think. Question it. You don't always believe what other people tell you or what you read in the papers, so why accept everything your thoughts tell you? You don't need to replace negative thoughts with positive ones, but you do need to start replacing them with more realistic ones. Realistic thoughts take into account the negative, but they also take into account the positive. For example, saying, "He didn't ask me out—I'm never going to be asked out," can be replaced by, "Okay, he didn't ask me out, but that doesn't mean there isn't someone out there who is right for me."

When negative thoughts start to appear, evaluate them carefully. Ask yourself if you are being realistic, and don't automatically treat your thoughts as facts just because you are thinking them. Look out for typical negative thought patterns, most of which are described next, and start challenging them.

## Tempest in a teacup

With tempest-in-a-teacup thinking, you exaggerate the negative effects of an event. Minor setbacks become major disasters. "I totally messed up" may refer to a tiny mistake, or an argument gets blown out of all proportion, becoming, in your thinking, full-out war. Exaggerating only makes you feel more out of your depth. Try to get into the habit of describing situations as they are and not exaggerating them. This will help you feel more in control. Okay, you made a mistake—we all do!

## I'm a failure—again

Everyone makes mistakes. In fact, the most interesting, exceptional people are the ones who make the most mistakes. The only way to learn about your strengths and your weaknesses is to make mistakes. Making mistakes builds character. Negative thinking can really slow you down when you are trying to achieve a goal or solve a problem. Every mistake you make will be interpreted as a failure and proof of your inadequacy. Of course failures can be devastating, but they can also help you grow and learn about yourself. You can gain something from every experience, however disappointing. Seen in this light, failures simply do not exist.

It's not what happens to you but how you react to what happens that determines your self-worth. If you failed an exam, find out what your weaknesses are and try again. Rather than labeling your mistakes or disappointments as failures, view them as setbacks or learning experiences that will add to your store of knowledge. Persistent effort pays off. Everywhere you turn there are examples of setbacks that later led to success. Walt Disney, Steven Spielberg, and J. K. Rowling are just a few examples of people whose ideas were initially rejected but who didn't give up and eventually achieved spectacular success. Just because things didn't go right the first time doesn't mean they never will. Perhaps you just need to try again or find another approach.

## It's never going to happen

Do you tend to think that once something has gone wrong once it will always go wrong? You have a bad day at work, and you decide the job's not for you, or one argument with a friend and the friendship is over. If you are prone to generalizing or drawing sweeping conclusions whenever you face a setback, you need to start challenging your thought patterns. Okay, you had a bad day at work, but you are still good at what you do. Okay, you had an argument with your friend, but this does not mean the friendship is over; you just need to sort out your differences. Nobody knows what the future holds. You may have a setback today, but it's entirely possible to work things out tomorrow.

## Blaming yourself

Negative thinkers always tend to blame themselves when things go wrong, but it's impossible to be in control of all the things that create a situation. If you tend to blame yourself, start examining all the factors involved in the setback, and you'll find that some of these may have nothing to do with you. Tell yourself, "Okay, this didn't happen, but how was I to know this or that would?" Get out of the habit of always taking the blame and telling yourself you aren't good enough. You may make mistakes, but you are still a worthwhile person.

## Fortune-telling

Some things are likely to happen. The sun will rise in the morning and set in the evening. At night the moon and stars will come out. But there is no such thing as complete certainty. The world probably won't, but it could end tomorrow. When you see only the negative, you lose a sense of perspective. You also forget that you are only human. You can't see into the future, and you can't know what is or is not going to happen. If you are prone to negative thinking, it's likely that your predictions always favor negative outcomes, but nobody can tell what the future holds. It's unlikely that everything will turn out wrong all the time. Your predictions are unrealistic and biased.

If you are prone to negative fortune-telling, start challenging that thinking now. If you think you know what people are thinking, question that assumption. You can never know for sure what someone else is thinking; you can only guess. It's more realistic to think that unpleasant things may or may not happen. It's more appropriate to conclude that someone is likely to think or do this, but you are not a mind reader. Things may turn out badly, but they may also turn out well. Allow yourself to think that things may turn out right, and get rid of over-the-top pessimism.

## Ignoring the positive

Ignoring the positive is the bleakest stage in the downward spiral of negative thinking. You don't think anything can go right anymore, and you want to give up. But life is full of disappointment and futility only if you think it is. I'm not asking you to focus totally on the positive and ignore the negative—that would be just as unrealistic!—but I am asking you to be more realistic. Okay, things could go wrong, but there is also the possibility they could go right. Life is a mixture of good and bad, and nothing is 100 percent negative. Negative thinking not only makes you feel unhappy and makes your life seem meaningless, it also is misleading and inaccurate.

## Worry

Worry is the state of mind that arises when negative thinking has taken hold. It's the sister of anxiety, when negative feelings have got

hold. When you worry, negative possibilities get magnified out of all proportion. We all have disturbing thoughts flying around in our heads from time to time, but you don't need to nurture them. Remember, you are in control of your thoughts. You may not be able to stop worry from happening—a certain amount of worry can be positive, as it highlights areas in your life where you need to make changes and move forward—but you can find ways to manage worry positively.

Just think of all the things you could be doing with that time wasted worrying. If you could harness that energy, imagine what you could be enjoying and how creative you could be. Your brain weighs just three pounds and produces enough energy to light a sixty-watt bulb, so use that energy to get more out of life.

The next time you start worrying, try the following:

- Stop and recognize that you are worrying. Try to identify what your worry is. If you don't know and just feel negative, see worry as a helpful warning sign that something in your life isn't working.
- If you stopped worrying completely, you would be of little value to yourself or anyone else. A certain amount of worry makes you feel better and gets you to check your actions, so do carry on worrying. However, did you know that 39 percent of the things you worry about never happen, 32 percent have already happened, 21 percent are trivial, and only 9 percent relate to issues with legitimate cause for concern? Concentrate on that 9 percent, and put the other 91 percent behind you. Learn to recognize what is important and what is not. Keep a worry notebook to help yourself worry constructively. Divide it into four sections, for things that might happen, things that have happened, small things to worry about today, important things to worry about.

- Ask yourself, "Is there anything I can do to change the situation?" If there is, get on and do it. Worrying about a problem does not solve it. Doing something about it does. If there isn't anything you can do, change your attitude to the situation and let your worry go.

- If you can't seem to let go of worry, find ways to distract yourself from it, such as exercise, reading, writing. Distraction isn't a solution, but it helps you come back with a fresh perspective.

- If worry is preventing you from making a decision, you need to think of all the possible alternatives, weigh the pros and cons, and take action. If you mess up, remind yourself that nobody can get it right all the time. Learn from the setback and try again.

- When you feel anxiety and worry taking over, do some deep breathing to relax your shoulders, neck, and face. Or you may prefer to use your imagination and imagine you yourself coping and handling difficult situations. Think about what you would say, how you would look, and what might happen. This tricks your mind into thinking you have dealt successfully with the situation you are worried about and gives you a series of contingency plans for all the different outcomes you can think of.

- Anchor yourself. Anchoring simply means associating positive, calming, confident feelings with an object you carry with you every day. Many people choose jewelry that they wear every day, but you could choose a finger or the back of your hand. In moments of strong negative emotions, touch your chosen object and focus on the feelings you have linked with it.

- Face your fear. The more you run away from things, the more powerful you make them by rendering yourself unable to deal with them. In life there is very little to fear apart from fear itself. Break the things you fear down into stages, and tackle each one independently. You can do it if you think you can.

## Smooth, Gentle, and Natural

It's time to start asking yourself questions again. Do you have any faulty or irrational beliefs that need to be replaced by more positive ones? Just as the wrong teapot can ruin the flavor of a cup of tea, wrong thinking can ruin your life. Make sure the pot you use is clean, has an appearance you like, and pours everything out smoothly, gently, and naturally—and make sure you are also comfortable with your thoughts. Do they make you feel good about yourself?

Nourishing Blend #4 sounds so simple, but in practice you may find it more of a challenge. The key is practice. You are learning a new skill. You are learning to talk to yourself in a reassuring and supportive way. Your negative thoughts aren't used to being challenged. Keep practicing, and positive thoughts will become second nature. You will start recognize when you are losing perspective, worrying too much, and soon the put-downs and negative assessments of your ability won't seem so compelling anymore. They may even start to seem melodramatic, unrealistic, and slightly absurd. You'll begin to realize just how much the quality of your life is affected by the quality of your thoughts. How you think about a situation or event determines a lot of how you feel and behave in that situation.

*While there's tea there's hope.*
—Sir Arthur Wing Pinero (1855–1934), British actor, playwright, and essayist

## The Power of a Positive Perspective

Some people always manage to think about situations in a way that leaves them feeling empowered and strong. They can take a negative situation and reframe it to find the positive. You can change your life

# What's Wrong with My Tea?

### Tasteless
The tea might have been stored too long. Buy little and often for a really good cup and to give you a chance to try many kinds of teas.

### Scummy
Most likely a poor-quality water problem. Try using bottled or filtered water instead.

### Dull and Flat
Simple. You're using poor-quality tea. Treat yourself to something better. Or perhaps you didn't boil the water before pouring or are using re-boiled water.

### Metallic
Either the tea or the water you are using is of poor quality.

### Bitter
Perhaps you have overmeasured the tea. It's always best to use less than you think you need. Or perhaps it has been brewed for too long.

### Cloudy
Unless you are using Assam (Assams can cream over and reflect the light), this could be poor-quality water or a poor-quality tea.

with the power of positive perspective. When you think of something in a negative way, you are limiting your options. Yes, something could go wrong, but then again, it could go right, or other options could open up to you. The art of thinking with a positive perspective is not about ignoring problems—remember, realism is important—but about being able to make your thoughts work for you.

As soon as thoughts of failure start to grind you down, keep your thinking flexible. Give yourself more choices, just as Thomas Edison did while trying to invent the lightbulb. Refusing to label himself a failure, even after seven hundred ideas failed, he told a reporter, "I have succeeded in proving that those seven hundred ways will not work. When I have eliminated all the ways that will not work, I will find the way that will work." Try using the power of positive perspective in your life. How could you think about a project to increase your chances of staying motivated?

Asking yourself questions is a powerful way to challenge negative thinking and open up a more positive perspective. If things are going wrong or you feel bad about yourself, ask yourself what you can do. Questions increase your range of options and encourage your brain to think less in black and white and more in color, to focus less on one possibility and more on a number of possibilities—and you always get more of what you focus on in life.

The way you think about yourself can mean the difference between success and failure, high and low self-esteem. In many ways what you believe has a far greater power than the truth. For example, for many centuries people believed that the world was flat and that they could fall off the horizon, so they didn't travel there.

Your thoughts really do have the power to determine the quality of your life. They are like lenses through which you view the world. If your lens is covered with bad thoughts about yourself and the world, what you see will be bad, but if you replace bad thoughts with more uplifting ones, the world will seem a friendlier, kinder place.

Your thoughts determine how you feel and the direction you will take in life. The way you see the world is a manifestation of the thoughts that you have in your mind. So what do you think of your life? Is your teacup always half-full no matter how empty it may

# How to Store Tea

Quality black teas can last up to two years after harvest in a vacuum pack or tin. But it is hard to know exactly when teas are harvested, and most teas travel by sea, sometimes for months, before they arrive in shops. In light of this, six months to a year is probably the maximum you should store black tea. Green teas and blended teas should last up to six months in storage.

When storing tea, store in a dark, airtight container with no risk of dampness or condensation, and keep the container away from spices and strong-smelling foods, as tea's flavor can be easily tainted.

---

seem to others? What kind of person do you think you are? Do you feel happy? Do you feel in control? Are you at peace with yourself?

If you aren't sure, Nourishing Blend #5 will be very important to you.

*Meanwhile, let us have a sip of tea. The afternoon glow is brightening the bamboos, the fountains are bubbling with delight, the soughing of the pines is heard in our kettle. Let us dream of evanescence and linger in the beautiful foolishness of things.*
—Kakuzo Okakura (1862–1913), Japanese writer

*One should clean out a room in one's home and place only a tea table and chair in the room with some boiled water and a fragrant tea. Afterward, sit comfortably and allow one's spirit to become tranquil, light, and natural.*
—Li Ri Hua (1368–1644), scholar during the Ming Dynasty

# Nourishing Blend № 5

## *make sure the taste is evenly distributed*

*About Tea:* When you serve tea, each cup you pour needs to taste the same and be the same temperature.

*About Life:* Find the right middle way. Restore balance to your life.

When tea is poured, with its taste evenly distributed in each cup, it becomes a symbol for harmony and reminds us of the importance of balance in all aspects of life. Take a look at your life. Are you striving for harmony, for balance, for the right middle way?

> *Better to be deprived of food for three days than tea for one.*
> —Chinese proverb

## Striving for Harmony

To look and feel your best, it's crucial that you pay attention to and strive for balance in all areas of your life. Happiness depends on a balance not only between giving and taking, as we saw in Nourishing Blend #1, but in all dimensions of life: physical, mental, emotional, and spiritual. Without balance you'll be likely to feel stressed out, unsettled, and restless. This is because what you do in one area of your life will affect other areas. Have a think. It's hard to be cheerful (emotional) or to work productively (mental) when you are feeling exhausted (physical). It also works the other way. When you feel in tune with yourself (spiritual), it's easier to focus on your friends and loved ones (emotional) and your work (mental).

If you focus too hard on one thing and neglect the other dimensions of life, you'll lose your bearings. As the sayings go, "Nothing overmuch," and "Balance and moderation in all things." If you aren't feeling at your best today, ask yourself:

Have I taken care of my health today?
How much mental activity have I had today?
Have I been in touch with my feelings today?
Have I had some time out today?

Discover where the imbalance lies, and then find ways to recreate balance in your life. A car needs regular tune-ups and oil changes, and in the same way, you need time out to refresh the best thing you've got going for yourself—you. You need time to relax and unstring the bow, time to treat yourself to some tender loving care. This is what a life of balance is all about.

The balance-yourself suggestions listed next include some helpful tips that you might want to refer to from time to time. They are all about helping you feel good so that you can deal more effectively with life. They will remind you of the importance of renewing and strengthening the four key areas of your life: your body, your mind, your heart, and your soul.

*On the hob was a little brass kettle, hissing and boiling; spread upon the floor was a warm, thick rug; before the fire was a folding-chair, unfolded and with cushions upon it, by the chair*

*was a small folding-table, unfolded, covered with a white cloth,*
*and upon it were spread small covered dishes, a cup and saucer,*
*and a tea-pot; on the bed were new, warm coverings, a curious*
*wadded silk robe, and some books. The little, cold, miserable*
*room seemed changed into Fairyland. It was actually warm*
*and glowing.*
—Frances Hodgson Burnett, *Sara Crewe; or What Happened*
*at Miss Minchin's*

## Your body

If you put the wrong gas in a car, it won't run smoothly. The same applies to you. If you eat things that are unsuitable, you won't feel your best, look your best, or perform your best. Make the decision to eat well from today on. Be aware of what you are putting into your body. Give yourself nothing but the best and healthiest food choices. Eat plenty of fresh vegetables and fruit, high-fiber carbohydrates, and a moderate amount of protein. Cut down on processed foods that are loaded with additives and preservatives, and avoid sugar, salt, alcohol, and saturated fat. Drink lots of water to clear out toxins. Eating well is a great way to boost your mood and well-being. If you have been eating foods that you know aren't good for you, try breaking the habit for just one day. Then build up to two days, and so on, until eating well and giving your body the best nutrients have become a habit that increases your feeling of general well-being. You don't have to cut out everything that you enjoy; remember that principle of balance again. Eat healthily most of the time—say 80 percent—and you can still enjoy foods that aren't quite so good for you the other 20 percent of the time.

As well as eating right, one of the quickest and easiest ways to feel good about yourself is to get regular exercise. Exercise releases feel-good chemicals called endorphins into your body. So why do so many of us avoid exercise? Because we make unrealistic promises in the keep-fit department and then feel bad about ourselves when we can't live up to them. So keep your goals achievable. You don't need daily gym visits or marathon runs. Begin with three 10-minute sessions each week, and build from there to half an hour or so five or six times a week. If you are not used to exercise, set small goals, such as walking short distances instead of driving or taking the stairs instead of the elevator. Small achievements will build your enthusiasm and motivation to increase the amount of exercise you do, and once you start to feel fitter and look better, there will be no stopping you.

Finally, lack of quality sleep can easily throw you off balance and make life seem more stressful than it should be. Don't panic if you aren't getting eight hours of sleep a night. Everyone has different sleep needs. The best indicator of sleep need is how you feel during the day. Are you alert, energetic, and able to concentrate? If you feel exhausted, irritable, and about to doze off all the time, you are not getting enough sleep. Try to establish regular sleeping and waking times so you have a sleeping pattern your body can adjust to. Make sure your bedroom is comfortable and quiet. Avoid heavy meals, exercise, and caffeine for a few hours before you go to bed. Relax as much as you can before you go to bed. Take a warm bath, listen to some soothing music, or have a gentle and calming herbal tea.

## Your mind

Don't neglect your mind. Keep using it. Look for something new: take advantage of every opportunity that comes your way. Keep pace with what is current. Continue to learn. Keep up with life. Find a mentor to inspire you. Stay in the mainstream.

Education needn't stop when you leave school. Keep learning and discovering all the time. Children have a natural interest in the world around them, but as we get older we lose this interest in life, and this can lead to fatigue and boredom and a closed mind. Re-awaken your interest in life by doing something new. An adventurous spirit encourages creativity, excitement, and good feelings about yourself and your life. Do something you haven't done before. Go to a concert to listen to music you don't normally listen to, sign up for an evening class, learn a new language, visit a place you have never been before, vary your routine. The possibilities are endless. When you do something new, you always feel more energetic and learn something new about yourself.

Finding and developing a hobby or a talent or special interest is a great way to use your mind and boost your chances of happiness. There are all kinds of things you may be good at. You may have a talent for reading, writing, or speaking. You may have a gift for organizing or a good memory or a talent for helping others. You may have music or leadership skills or enjoy collecting stamps. It doesn't matter where your interests lie; when you do something you like, it's a form of self-expression. It's fun, it sharpens your mind, and it builds your self-esteem.

## Your heart

Who's running your life? For happy, contented living, it's important to be aware of the influence feelings have on your life. Otherwise they could end up running your life, and that all-important sense of balance will be lost. We've all been there—we know what's the right thing to do, but our feelings take over and we do something else. For example, someone cuts in front of you in traffic and you react badly, and for a moment expressing your anger is more important than driving safely. There are things you can do to improve the way you handle your feelings so that they don't start running your life.

The first thing to remember is just to let feelings be. You may not always be able to understand why you are feeling a certain way.

Sometimes, for instance, you just feel sad. Instead of fighting it and denying it or letting it spoil your day, simply acknowledge that you are feeling sad. You may find it hard to express painful emotions, but feelings, even the so-called negative ones, like sadness and anger, serve an important purpose in our lives. They are there to alert us to areas of discomfort in our lives. When feelings are not acknowledged, they cause even greater stress because we are not allowing ourselves to feel what is true for us. Emotions are messages from our inner wisdom. Listen to them. If they are not worked through or acknowledged, the biochemical effect of suppressed emotions may cause physical and emotional distress.

Emotions are the only real way we have to show what matters to us in life and what doesn't. Difficult emotions signal the need for some kind of change in our lives. They require us to act to change the situation or mindset that is causing distress. Negative emotions are not bad emotions; they are there so that we can recognize our needs and grow and develop.

Reconnecting with your emotions won't be easy if you have been used to denying or suppressing them, but it is important that you start to become more aware of what you are feeling. The next time you relax with a cup of tea, or anytime during the day, ask yourself how you are feeling. Stop and listen to your feelings, and accept them even if they are troublesome or difficult.

The next step is to choose how to respond to that emotion. In many cases you may wish to use a strategy to induce a state of calm within yourself. For instance, if you feel sad, you may find it helps to talk to a friend, spend time alone, or have a good cry. Choosing how to manage your feelings can be very empowering. It reminds you that you are the one in control. Feelings are powerful, but they can't make you do anything unless you allow them to.

And when everything seems to be going wrong or you feel really bad about yourself, keep your heart healthy and strong with the magic of laugher. Sometimes life sucks, and there isn't anything you can do about it, so you may as well have a good laugh.

## Your soul

When we forget to pay attention to our soul, we become nervous, stressed, and afraid. We are all creatures of the Earth, and the world will offer us support and calm if we take the time to connect with it and feed our soul.

One of the most effective ways to calm your mind is to get in touch with nature. Plan to escape to the country or a park, if only for a few hours a week. Take time to appreciate the wonders of nature, the color of the sky, the green of the grass, the song of the birds. Slow down for a while, and enjoy the peace and quiet. It's surprising how quickly you can restore yourself in this way. Feeling low is often the result of trying too hard to keep up with the pressures of modern life and neglecting your soul. Take a natural break, enjoy the simple pleasures, and find your center.

Another way to relax and feel calm is to become aware of your breathing, and allow it to slow down until you feel calmer. Close your eyes, and breathe deeply from your stomach. When you are ready, open your eyes and bring yourself slowly back into the room.

To lead a balanced life with inner strength and self-esteem, you sometimes need to stop doing and just *be*. Just being releases tension and increases self-awareness. Spend a few moments each day in total silence. Turn off the TV or radio. Don't read a book or do anything. This will be difficult at first, so try it for only a short time. As you get used to it, you will be able to do it for longer and balance your being with your doing.

# Complete Dedication

All five types of taste can be found in green tea: bitter, sweet, astringent, salty, and a fifth one that is hard to describe (sour?). In earlier years, in both China and Korea, when a new wife moved to her husband's house she would first make an offering of green tea to his ancestors. She did this because the tea symbolically represented, through its five tastes, all the various sufferings in life. In this way she completely dedicated herself to her husband's family.

# The Tea Taster

A small, exact amount of leaves is weighed out on scales. The brewing mug is filled with water, the lid put on, and the tea left to brew. After five minutes the tea is poured into a china bowl in front of a row of mugs that are laid out on a long table. As the taster walks down the line, he or she slurps and spits the tea, pulling closer the tastier bowls and pushing away the less desirable ones. A busy tea broker may taste hundreds of teas a day. It's an important task, because with tea, no two days are the same: taste varies slightly with each day's picking.

Learning to just be and to find an inner peace is crucial for a balanced and happy life. We discuss it more later, but for now just bear in mind that every time you make a cup of tea, put your feet up, and truly savor the moment, you are nourishing your soul.

## A Time for Everything

For the ancient tea masters, the drinking of tea demonstrates to people how to proceed in their evolution as human beings. This Way of Tea is one of the "right middle ways," that is, the way of equanimity and harmony. As the tea infuses in the pot, the bitterness remains at the bottom with the leaves, and as the tea is poured, each serving becomes progressively more bitter. To equalize the taste, during the second round of pouring you need to fill the cups in reverse order so the taste is evenly distributed.

The principle of balance and harmony symbolically and beautifully represented in the ancient tea ceremony reminds us of the importance of finding the right middle way and balancing all aspects of our lives. Of course, in real life this isn't always going to be possible. Sometimes you will need to push yourself to the limit. Sometimes you will need to get angry. Sometimes you won't have time to exercise and eat right. That's okay; that's life. There is a time for everything—a time to be balanced and a time to be imbalanced—as long as you remember also to take time for renewal.

If you go too hard for too long or neglect an area of your life for too long, you won't think as clearly, you'll get moody, and you'll lose a sense of perspective. You may think you don't have time to eat right, sleep right, build friendships, or get inspired. In reality you don't have time not to. The downtime you spend restoring balance to your life will pay you back, because every time you take a step back and adjust your pace, the quality of your life improves beyond imagining.

*My dear, if you could give me a cup of tea to clear my muddle of a head I should better understand your affairs.*
—Charles Dickens

# Be Your Own Tea Taster

Look at the leaves. Are they large or small? In most cases, the larger and more even-sized the leaf, the better the quality.

What do the tea and the wet leaves smell like? The aroma should be released as soon as the tea is poured.

Look at the tea. It should be fresh and bright with a golden halo around the edge of the cup.

Take a sip of tea, and, keeping the tea in your mouth, suck in air through your teeth with a slurping noise. Does the taste reflect the tea's aroma? How much body can you feel? If you are tasting more than two teas, spit this mouthful out instead of swallowing it.

Develop your own tea-tasting vocabulary to help you identify characteristics and flavors. For example, good characteristics might be bright, fragrant, full-bodied, and pungent. Bad might be thick, harsh, cloudy, or scummy. Good flavors might be flowery, misty, astringent, and brisk. Bad might be dull, soft, flat, and soapy.

# Tea-Tasting Terminology

**Autumnal:** Late-season tea from Assam and Darjeeling (September to October)

**Astringent:** Term for mouth-drying quality of green tea or lightly fermented black tea—not in the least bit derogatory

**Bakery:** Characteristic of an overfired black tea from which too much moisture has been removed

**Biscuity:** A pleasant aroma; often used to describe quality Assams

**Bright:** Suggesting good color and good quality; a clean, fresh taste

**Brisk:** Often used to describe the freshness of good-quality, well-manufactured tea

**Burnt:** Taste of tea that has been fired too long

**Chesty:** A slightly dull, woody taste that some teas develop because of time spent in a tea chest or poor picking and grading

**Colory:** A bright, attractive color

**Common:** A plain, thick tea that has no distinct flavor or characteristics

**C.T.C.:** Cut, torn, and curled: tea leaves that have been machine processed for tea bags

**Flat:** Tea that is no longer fresh

**Flush:** A period of growth during the seasonal cycle of a tea bush. Most commonly used for Darjeeling's best teas; the first-flush tea is the first harvest of the year in February-March; the second flush starts in early April and is the main crop

**Full:** Describes a good combination of round, smooth color and strength

**Hard:** A pungent green tea with a harsh, bitter taste

**Harsh:** Tea that has been underwithered, resulting in a rough taste

**Light:** Tea that lacks color, body, aroma, and strength

**Liquor:** Term used for brewed tea

**Malty:** A desirable quality commonly found in Assam teas—like brewer's malt

**Metallic:** A sharp, coppery flavor found in some black teas

**Muscat:** A black currantish flavor and aroma common to fine Darjeelings

**Pungent:** A positive word for clean, fresh tea

**Self-drinker:** What the tea blender calls a tea that is good enough to be drunk by itself; it does not need blending

**Smoky:** Characteristic flavor of some Chinese teas, such as Lapsang souchong; if found in other teas, it is undesirable and usually caused by leaks around the dryer heating tubes during processing

**Stale:** Faded aroma and a dead taste caused by age and loss of quality due to age

**Tannin:** Naturally present in all leaves and wood, it contributes to the dry taste in the mouth; becomes bitter in tea that has been dried too quickly

**Thin:** Light tea lacking any strong or desirable characteristics

**Toasty:** Aroma of a fine Keemun or other highly fired tea

**Weedy:** Grassy or haylike taste caused by underwithering; may also be a woody taste

**Winy:** Refers to aging of tea, which doesn't enhance flavor, as it does with wine. Exceptions to this rule are fine Keemuns or Darjeelings, for which aging may bring out a mellow characteristic

# Nourishing Blend № 6
## *time is of the essence*

About Tea: Nothing is worse than an oversteeped cup of tea. Time is of the essence. Great tea requires you to take your time as well as keep your eye on the clock.

About Life: Enjoy today, but keep an eye on tomorrow.

To make the perfect cup of tea, you need to be patient but also to keep your eye on the clock. You need to be able to manage time. As you'll see in this chapter, the ability to appreciate and manage time is crucial not only for great tea, but also for a harmonious and fulfilled life.

There is no more precious gift than the days and minutes of our existence; just ask anyone who has had a brush with death. But for many of us time is not a precious gift but a deadly enemy that we are constantly trying to defeat. We want to rush time so that we can do what we like. We want to beat time so we can accomplish everything on the list, enjoy the good times, and avoid the inevitability of aging. We need to ask ourselves two questions: Where does our time go, and what are we doing with this precious gift?

*A Little Princess . . . it's always tea-time. . . .*
—Lewis Carroll, *Alice in Wonderland*

# Where Does Our Time Go and What Are We Doing with This Precious Gift?

If you've ever tried to lose weight, you may have kept a food journal to record the food you eat. You began by thinking that you hardly ate a thing, but keeping the journal revealed that you actually ate far more than you thought. It's the same with time. We think we know why we never have enough time for the things that matter to us, but in reality we don't. Assessing how you spend your time can help you change the way you spend time to better reflect who you are and what matters to you.

So track your time, just as a dieter might track food consumption. Try it for one day, and see where your time goes. Write down in a journal how you spend your time when you wake up, what you do during the day, and so on. Include things like how long it takes you to find lost car keys, get dressed, read a paper. Nothing is too small to note. This type of record tells you at a glance how you actually spend your time.

Pick a time when you aren't stressed or tired, and focus on what you have recorded. Read it through carefully, and listen to your internal voice. Are there moments of happiness and fulfillment in your present experience? You'll be surprised at what you discover. Perhaps you are looking to the big goals in your life to offer satisfaction, but what you may find is that the great joys in life are often found in tiny, unexceptional moments of your day.

Now take time to identify the misfits in your life. For each item in your daily life, ask two questions: Does this contribute to my health and happiness? Does it have to be done now? If you get two yeses, that item probably deserves to be a priority in your life. But if you get a no—"No, this is time trouble"—it deserves one more question and a ruthlessly honest answer: Why do I give my time to this?

# Taking Your Time with Tea

Taste is always subjective, so it is impossible to give exact steeping times for tea. However, nothing is worse than an oversteeped cup of tea. It tastes bitter and like gravy. To avoid this, it might be a good idea to keep timers in the place where you normally steep tea. How many minutes should you set your timers for? Generally, 3 to 5 minutes should be sufficient, but steeping guidelines vary according to the tea's color, style, and grade. Tea bags are designed for ease and speed, so they require very little time. Full, large-leafed high-grade oolongs probably take the most time because they have less surface contact with water.

As a rough guide, the steeping times for black teas are between 3 and 5 minutes. Oolong teas take 4 to 7 minutes. Steep green teas for 2 to 3 minutes. Herbal teas may take 5 to 7 minutes. Delicate white teas steep for around 2 minutes, while first-flush Darjeelings take 2 to 5 minutes. Tea bags can be as little as 30 seconds. Again, these are all guidelines, and personal taste should dictate how long to extract specific teas.

## Get Rid of Time Misfits

Time misfits take many forms, but they have one thing in common: they take up time that could be better spent elsewhere. Identifying them goes a long way toward robbing them of their power over your life. Time misfits are things that don't need to be done, at least by you. They may be habits or false politeness, such as attending a function you don't want to attend because you were invited or staying on the phone too long with a friend when there really isn't any more to say. Time misfits are really personal—what is a misfit to one person may add joy to another's time—but some are universal, such as watching hours of TV, opening junk mail, unnecessary reorganizing, or changing clothes several times a day.

Begin by identifying the time wasters in your day, and start tackling them one at a time. Try not doing a time waster for one day, then continue not doing it for a week, then a month, until you stop doing it altogether. Then tackle the next time waster. Perhaps you don't need to stop doing these things completely; they just need to take up less time, and you just need to do them more efficiently or delegate them or do them less often. For example, could the kids not help more with chores? Could you make do with twice-a-week instead of daily trips to the supermarket? With better planning, you can save money, fuel, wear and tear, and time.

Finally, there are time misfits you need to identify that you won't find in your journal. These are habits of thought and attitude that eat your time without you even knowing it. They are unconscious companions that carry off priceless hours without adding anything to the quality of your life. Most of us lose an enormous amount of precious time to worry. As you saw in Nourishing Blend #5, worry is usually based on what might happen, not on reality, and when you worry you achieve nothing. If you are anxious about the future, you need to discover if you can take action and then take it. The rest is wasted time.

Negativity in one form or another also eats the heart out of your time. It may take the shape of anger, when we waste our creativity planning revenge. It may take the shape of jealousy, when we waste energy comparing ourselves with others. It may be fear, self-doubt, fear of failure, or guilt. No matter what form negativity takes, it stops us from enjoying time and the best that life can offer.

## Reinventing time

Now that you've begun to think about how you spend your time and you've taken steps to change aspects of it that work against you, you are ready to invent a life that makes the most of the time you have been given. Give your best time first to who or what really matters to you. What are your best times in a given day? When are you most creative? If you're a morning person, do your creative work then instead of using that time for errands and chores. Stop spending your prime time doing things you could do in your off-peak hours. Educate friends and loved ones that you are not available then. Make sure you block off enough time for sleeping, eating, reflecting, and any other components of personal health and also enough time for travel, study, work, and so on. With a will to change, you can make the most of the time you have—not to fit more in but to live the way you want to live.

## One sip at a time

Your next task is to practice doing one activity at a time, to find the joy of being where you are and doing what you want to do. No matter what you are doing, if you give it your full attention, the quality of your time increases considerably. Are you drinking your tea? Then notice the steam rising from the cup. Concentrate on the warmth and energy as you swallow your tea one sip at a time. Are you opening your mail? Focus on the letters. Imagine who would have sent them and how they would have pictured you receiving it. Focus on one activity at a time.

## Prepare for the unexpected

It's important to choose how you spend your time, but you also need to prepare for the unexpected. Sometimes it's hard to focus completely when there are distractions and unexpected interruptions. Don't be surprised if life doesn't always go as planned, and be prepared to make adjustments; otherwise you'll end up feeling frustrated and defeated, which isn't a productive way to spend your time. The trick is to recognize what is unavoidable or desirable, requiring you to be flexible, and what is an unnecessary imposition, requiring you to be firm.

## Plan to play

Make sure you give recreation—playtime—as much focus and attention as any other activity in your life. If you've been indoctrinated by a money-hungry, work-obsessed society, this may not come easily, but study after study has shown that the key to happy, productive living is including playtime. If you skimp on fun or rest or holidays, you'll crush your spirit and your motivation. A guilt-free approach to having fun helps us to stop postponing life and to enjoy time in all its fullness.

## Plan for potential time

And finally, save time for reflection—for discovering the potential in your life and yourself. You may feel you haven't got time for it, but even thirty minutes is enough to give you a sense of perspective before charging ahead. We'll explore this in more detail later, but for now bear in mind that time saved for reflection is time well spent, as it can add valuable insight, joy, and balance to your daily experience.

## Lost in time

Wonderful, aren't they, those fleeting moments in life when you lose track of time or time stands still? These moments are, in essence, time of the highest quality. Uncomplicated by disruptions, they occur when we are most in tune with ourselves. Great athletes

# Savoring Time

Sen Rikyū, the sixteenth-century tea master who perfected the Way of Tea, was once asked to explain what this Way entails. He replied that it was a matter of observing but seven rules: make a satisfying bowl of tea; lay the charcoal so that the water boils efficiently; provide a sense of warmth in the winter and coolness in the summer; arrange the flowers as though they were in the field; be ready ahead of time; be prepared in case it should rain; act with utmost consideration toward your guests.

According to the well-known story relating the dialogue between Rikyu and the questioner who asked about the Way, the questioner was vexed by Rikyu's reply, saying that those were simple matters that anyone could handle. To this, Rikyu responded that he would become a disciple of the person who could carry them out without fail.

This story tells us that the Way of Tea is concerned with activities that are a part of everyday life, yet to master these requires great cultivation. In this sense, the Way of Tea is well described as the Art of Living.

As seen in Rikyu's seven rules, the Way of Tea requires creating the proper setting for enjoying that moment with a perfect bowl of tea. Everything that goes into that serving of tea, even the quality of the air and the space where it is served, becomes a part of its flavor. The perfect tea must therefore capture the "flavor" of the moment—the spirit of the season, of the occasion, of the time and the place. The event called *chaji*, "a full tea gathering," is where this takes place and where the Way of Tea unfolds as an exquisite, singular moment in time shared and savored fully by the participants.

*When you place a tea utensil, you should withdraw your hand as though it were a loved one you were leaving.*
—Sen Rikyū (1522–1591), Japanese tea master who perfected the tea ceremony

experience them in the midst of a game brilliantly played. Artists find them at the height of their creative powers, when the muse strikes and art and spirit become one. Teachers feel them when they see the lights come on in the eyes of their pupils. Lovers and parents feel them in the blessed space of true, undiverted intimacy.

You are lost in time whenever you are totally absorbed in a task or a person or a thought. It's as if you have forgotten time and thus become a part of it. Often these moments, like happiness, come when you least expect them, but this doesn't mean you shouldn't expect them. If you create a life for yourself in which what you value shapes what you do and with whom you spend your time, then timelessness and harmony will follow.

> *One should drink tea while appreciating the fragrance of the flowers, the brightness of the moon, the beauty of music. After drinking tea one will no longer be in a daze but feel as frank and as open as heaven and earth.*
> —Seng-Jiao Ran (720–799), Chinese monk of the Tang Dynasty

## Looking Ahead

One of the few things you can never recycle is wasted time. So make sure you treasure every moment, but at the same time you also need to keep an eye on tomorrow. Why? Because thinking beyond today can be quite exciting and can help you take charge of the present.

Just as you need to set a timer to make sure your tea is brewed correctly, you also need to set goals and plan ahead. If you do things just as they pop into your head, your life can lack direction and focus, and you will be prone to wasting time. The actions you choose to focus on today will shape your tomorrow.

# Tea and Its Times

Where did it all begin? According to Chinese mythology, in 2737 BC the Chinese Emperor, Shen Nung, a scholar and herbalist, was sitting beneath a tree while his servant boiled drinking water. A leaf from the tree dropped into the water, and Shen Nung decided to try the brew. The tree was a wild tea tree.

From the earliest times, tea was renowned for its properties as a healthy, refreshing drink. By the third century AD, many stories were being told and some written about tea and the benefits of tea drinking, but it was not until the Tang Dynasty (AD 618–906) that tea became China's national drink and the word *ch'a* was used to describe tea.

The first book on tea, *Ch'a Ching,* written about the year 780, was written by the Chinese author Lu Yu. It comprises three volumes and covers tea from its growth through to its making and drinking, as well as including a historical summary and famous early tea plantation.

As Buddhist priests start to move through China and Japan, the cultivation and drinking of tea followed them. The Indian and Japanese legends both attribute it to Bodhidharma, the devout Buddhist priest who founded Zen Buddhism. The Indian legend tells how in the fifth year of a seven-year sleepless contemplation of Buddha, Bodhidharma began to feel drowsy. He immediately plucked a few leaves from a nearby bush and chewed them, and thus dispelled his tiredness. The bush was a wild tea tree.

The first mention of tea outside China and Japan is said to be by the Arabs in AD 850, and it was they who brought it to Europe by way of the Venetians, circa 1559. However, it is the Portuguese and Dutch who claim the credit for bringing tea and tea drinking to Europe.

The Portuguese opened up the sea routes to China, some say as early as 1515. Jesuit priests traveling on the ships brought the tea-drinking habit back to Portugal, while the sailors manning the ships encouraged the Dutch merchants to enter the trade. Subsequently, a regular shipment of tea to ports in France, Holland, America, and the Baltic coast was set up in 1610. England entered the trade via the East India Company, or the John Company as it was known, in the mid- to late-seventeenth century.

# Boston Tea Party

The Boston Tea Party is famous in the history of American independence. As an early example of American rebellion against British rule, it represents one of the significant events leading ultimately to the American Revolution.

On December 16, 1773, between thirty and sixty men disguised as Native Americans boarded ships owned by the British East India Company. Once aboard, they smashed open the tea cargoes from wooden chests and threw them into the sea. Washed up on shore next morning, the cargo was of course worthless. Settlers at other ports followed suit, and every patriotic American gave up tea drinking and turned to coffee.

So what led to this incident? The British government at the time was levying tax on imported products such as tea to raise money for the military and other government services. At that time, tea drinking was as popular in the American colonies as it was in Britain. Americans were outraged by the imposition by Lord North of tax on tea in both Britain and America as well as the lack of American representation in the British Parliament, giving rise to the famous slogan, "No taxation without representation."

At the same time, the Tea Act of 1773 gave the East India Company the right to ship tea from China directly to America. This was enacted to counter the American practice of buying (and sometimes smuggling) tea in from Holland and even directly from China via the Dutch, a practice that reduced trade for the East India Company. This law put many American tea importers out of business, as they incurred a tax the locals didn't want. The Americans decided that the British had interfered once too often, and the Boston Tea Party took place.

History shows that tea drinking was once very popular in the United States, and as the centuries roll by it is once again growing in popularity, with Americans leading the trends for specialty teas, like Pu-erh tea and iced tea.

Let's have a look ahead, using the tool of your imagination. Find a place where you can be alone without interruption.

There, now clear your mind of everything. Don't worry about work, money, or the kids; just focus and breathe deeply and open your mind. In your mind's eye, see someone walking toward you about half a block away. At first you can't see who it is. As this person gets closer, you suddenly realize it's you. But it's not the you of today. It's you as you would like to be in two years' time. Now think deeply. What have you done with your time in the last two years? How do you feel about your life? What do you look like?

You can float back to reality now, and if you actually tried the experiment, you probably got in touch with your deeper self. You got a feel of what matters to you in life and what's important to you and what you want to accomplish over the next two years. That's called looking ahead, and it's a powerful tool for turning your dreams into a reality.

Use constructive time management procedures to make sure you achieve those goals. Plan your day's activities. Construct a plan for the week, month, year, or five or ten years ahead. Although we have only the here and now, scheduling in the present for what we plan to do in the future helps us to stay on top of work and play. Otherwise, time is wasted with shoulds, coulds, and oughts, and we never get to develop our full potential. Be knowledgeable about the responsibilities and opportunities before you. Plan ahead with flexibility, but do plan ahead.

Looking ahead isn't about neglecting the present; it is about seizing the day so that your life is as fulfilling and rewarding as possible. Whatever your hopes and dreams for the future, since the future is unwritten, why not do all you can now to ensure it is extraordinary and you leave a lasting legacy?

# Looking Ahead with Tasseography

Reading tea leaves is a form of divination that relies on the tea-leaf reader's intuitive ability to interpret the different symbols and patterns created by loose tea leaves in a cup.

To read someone's tea leaves, you must prepare a cup of tea with loose tea leaves. A small, white cup with no designs or patterns on the inside walls is ideal. Drink your tea, and leave a tiny amount of liquid, as well as some tea leaves, in the bottom of the cup. Holding the cup in your left hand, slowly swirl the contents of the cup around three times clockwise. Try to make sure that the leaves are moved toward the rim of the teacup. Then place the cup upside down on a saucer, holding it there for a few seconds while letting the fluids drain. When the teacup is placed right side up again, make sure the handle faces toward you, and take a look at the patterns made by the tea leaves remaining in the cup.

If you have swirled correctly, the leaves should now be clumped together in several different places on the cup's inside, including the rim, sides, and bottom. These clumps will form the symbols that you will read. You should always begin the interpretation by looking for the simplest symbols first. Several of the leaf clumps may clearly form shapes, letters, or numbers.

**Shapes:** Triangles = good karma; Squares = need for caution; Circles = great success; Heart = love; Triangle = jealousy
**Letters:** May refer to the names of friends or relatives
**Numbers:** Can indicate spans of time, like months or years

Most of the clumps, however, will form random shapes. With a little staring and a bit of creativity, these shapes can easily be distinguished. Here are some guidelines and fairly obvious traditional meanings of some symbols you might see to help you get started, but remember, the beauty of tea-leaf reading is that it is entirely up to your creativity.

**Acorn:** At the top, success and gain; at the bottom, good health
**Aircraft:** Journey; if broken, danger of an accident; can mean a rise in position

*continued*

**Anchor:** Rest, stability, constancy; clouded, inconstancy
**Apple:** Achievement
**Axe:** Difficulties; near the top, difficulties overcome
**Baby:** Small worries
**Bag:** A trap; if open, escape
**Ball:** Variable fortunes
**Bell:** Unexpected news; good if near the top
**Birds:** Good news
**Boat:** Visit from a friend, protection
**Book:** Open, good news; closed, a need to investigate something
**Bush:** New friends or opportunities; something growing in life
**Butterfly:** Fickleness
**Cabbage:** Jealousy; with dots, at work
**Candle:** Help from others
**Cap:** Trouble, take care
**Cat:** Deceit, a false friend
**Chain:** Engagement, a wedding
**Chair:** A guest
**Cigar:** New friends
**Circle:** Success, completion; with a dot, a baby
**Clock:** Better health
**Clouds:** Trouble; with dots, many problems
**Coin:** Money coming
**Comb:** An enemy
**Cross:** Suffering, sacrifice
**Cup:** Reward
**Dagger:** Danger from self or others; beware of recklessness
**Dish:** Trouble at home
**Dog:** Good friend; if at bottom, friend needs help
**Door:** Odd event
**Duck:** Money coming
**Egg:** Good omen
**Elephant:** Wisdom and strength

*continued*

**Envelope:** Good news
**Eye:** Caution
**Face:** A change, may be a setback
**Fan:** Flirtation
**Feather:** Lack of concentration
**Fence:** Limitations, minor setbacks, not permanent
**Finger:** Emphasizes whatever sign it points at
**Fire:** Achievement, especially artistic; danger of haste
**Fish:** Good fortune
**Flag:** Danger
**Fly:** Domestic annoyance
**Fork:** False flattery
**Forked Line:** Decision
**Fruit:** Prosperity
**Gate:** Opportunity, future success
**Glass:** Integrity
**Glow:** A challenge
**Goat:** Be careful of enemies
**Grapes:** Happiness
**Gun:** Quarrels, anger
**Hammer:** Hard work needed
**Hand:** If open, friendship; if closed, an argument
**Harp:** Love, harmony
**Hat:** Improvement, especially a new job
**Hawk:** Jealousy
**Heart:** Love, pleasure, trust
**Horn:** Abundance
**Horse:** If galloping, good news; if head only, a lover
**Horseshoe:** Good luck
**Hourglass:** Need to decide something
**House:** Security
**Iceberg:** Danger
**Insect:** Problems are minor and easily overcome
**Jewels:** Gifts
**Kangaroo:** Harmony at home

**Kettle:** Any illness is minor
**Kite:** Wishes coming true
**Knife:** Broken friendship
**Ladder:** Promotion, a rise in life
**Lamp:** At top, a feast; at side, secrets revealed; at bottom, a feast or a party postponed
**Leaf:** Good fortune, new life
**Letter:** News
**Lines:** Straight, progress; wavy, uncertain path
**Lion:** Influential friends
**Lock:** Obstacles
**Loop:** Avoid impulsive action
**Man:** A visitor; clear and distinct
**Mask:** Excitement; insecurity
**Mountain:** Great goals, but also difficulties
**Mouse:** Theft
**Mushroom:** At top, journey or move to the country; near bottom, rapid growth, but if reversed, frustration
**Nail:** Injustices, unfairness
**Necklace:** Complete, admirers; broken, danger of losing a lover
**Needle:** Recognition, admiration
**Oak:** Health, long life
**Octopus:** Danger
**Ostrich:** Travel
**Owl:** Gossip, scandal
**Palm Tree:** Success, honor
**Parasol:** New lover
**Parrot:** A journey, but also people talking
**Pig:** Prosperity, possibly greed
**Pistol:** Danger
**Purse:** At top, profit; at bottom, loss
**Question Mark:** Need for caution
**Rabbit:** Need for bravery
**Rake:** Watch details
**Raven:** Bad news

*continued*

**Ring:** At top, marriage or an offer of marriage; at bottom, long engagement; if broken, engagement is broken off
**Rose:** Popularity
**Saw:** Interference
**Scale:** Legal issues; if balanced a just result; if unbalanced, unjust
**Scissors:** Quarrels, possibly separation
**Sheep:** Good fortune
**Shell:** Good news
**Shelter:** Danger of loss or ill health
**Ship:** Worthwhile journey
**Shoe:** Change for the better
**Snake:** An enemy, but also wisdom
**Spider:** Reward for work
**Spoon:** Generosity
**Star:** Health and happiness, hope
**Sun:** Happiness, success, power
**Sword:** Arguments
**Table:** Social gathering
**Tent:** Travel
**Thimble:** Changes at home
**Tortoise:** Criticism, usually beneficial
**Tower:** Disappointments
**Tree:** Improvements
**Triangle:** Something unexpected
**Umbrella:** Annoyances
**Urn:** Wealth and happiness
**Vase:** A friend who needs help
**Violin:** Egotism
**Volcano:** Harmful emotions
**Wagon:** A wedding
**Wasp:** Romantic problems
**Waterfall:** Prosperity
**Wheel:** If complete, good fortune; if broken, disappointments

**Wings:** Messages
**Wolf:** Jealousy
**Yoke:** Domination
**Zebra:** Adventure, especially overseas

After a few readings, you will become more and more adept at assigning names to symbols and in doing so will be able to interpret just about anything. Remember that the most important thing in reading tea leaves is your own creativity.

## The Perfect Cup

Perhaps the most important thing to remember, if you want to make great tea, is that tea requires its devotees to take their time. Take the time to learn how you like your tea, and take the time to steep it well to perfection and to drink it. And perhaps the most important thing to remember, if you want to lead a happy life, is that life offers no more precious gift than the days and hours and minutes and seconds of our existence. So count each day as a gift; that's why it's called the present. And if you can enjoy today and keep an eye on tomorrow, one day you'll realize that you are making the perfect cup and living the perfect life . . . for you.

# Nourishing Blend № 7

## *make and serve a delicious cup of tea*

*About Tea:* Prepare, serve, and drink your chosen tea. Appreciate the remarkable tastes, flavors, and healing properties of tea.

*About Life:* Put your heart into everything you do.

Many rituals and traditions are connected with the enjoyment of tea. From the profoundly intricate Japanese tea ceremony to Chinese tea-drinking customs, tea drinking becomes a spiritual event. To the uninitiated, tea ceremonies are beautiful occasions, but to those who follow the Way of Tea they are a path toward an enlightened life. The ceremonies are complex and intricate and take a number of different forms depending on country of origin, but they all teach humility, discipline, loving attention to detail, however small, and an adoration of the beautiful and pure in everyday things.

## Are You True to Yourself?

Seemingly simple rules govern every detail of the tea ceremony to ensure that only the very best tea is served and the enjoyment of the guests is maximized. Cleanliness, hygiene, purity, and harmony are also highlighted. All this reminds us of the importance of putting our hearts into everything we do and being true to ourselves.

Do you remember the self-awareness exercises we did in Nourishing Blend #3? They were designed to get you thinking about the kind of person you are. Let's take this one stage further and ask if you are being true to yourself. If you aren't sure, ask yourself one question: Are you putting your heart into everything you do? If the answer is no or not sure, then you need to learn how to get back to the real you and find your deep inner conviction.

What would happen to your life today if you took everything out of your life that didn't ring true to who you are and to your heart? It isn't an impossible dream. Transforming your life in this incredible way depends on knowing who you are and what you value. For many of us, the answers to these questions have become a bit vague. We have accepted other people's valuations and expectations of us and along the way have lost sight of ourselves, or we are so busy that our sense of self is lost in the mad rush. So how do you get back to the real you?

First of all, you need to slow down and create some individual space to get reacquainted with yourself. You don't need to go on retreat; just small changes in your routine will do. Give yourself a break from television, radios, phones, and the newspaper for a couple of hours, and don't fill the space with something else. Advise friends and family that you're not available then, and find a place to be alone, even if it means taking yourself out for a cup of tea or for lunch. Taking yourself out can open yourself to the insight that comes from the simple but neglected act of observing life as it bustles around you. If possible, book a day off, and spend the time reflecting and thinking about what matters to you. You might want to keep a journal to preserve a record of your thoughts and feelings. It doesn't matter how long you spend at it or how you take time out, the important thing is that solitary reflection becomes a necessary and treasured part of your life.

Once you've gotten into the habit of taking time out, start thinking about what really matters to you. You might want to write a personal mission statement in which you describe your own vision. You might want to develop a top-ten list of who or what matters in your life and then think about how your life reflects the importance of the items on the list. You might want to interview yourself. What questions would you ask yourself, and how would you respond?

Start getting into the habit of recognizing the choices you make in your daily life. Every day consists of a myriad of choices, from whether to get out of bed or doze for another hour to whether to read the paper or take a brisk walk. Every part of our daily lives is in fact a choice, even though we may not realize it, since we often get bogged down with reactive language, such as "I can't" or "That's the way it is." Try distinguishing between proactive and reactive language. Replace "I can't" with "Let's look at other options," or "If only" with "I will." Only when you can recognize and take responsibility for the choices you make can you stop being reactive and move on to leading a conscious, intentional life.

> *When all is complete deep in the teapot, when tea, mint, and sugar have completely diffused throughout the water, coloring and saturating it, . . . then a glass will be filled and poured back into the mixture, blending it further. Then comes waiting. Motionless waiting. Finally, from high up, like some green cataract whose sight and sound mesmerize, the tea will once again cascade into a glass. Now it can be drunk, dreamily, forehead bowed, fingers held wide away from the scalding glass.*
> —Simone Jacquemard, *Le mariage berbère*

We live so much of our lives on autopilot and find ourselves doing things without thinking or feeling. To live proactively, you have to turn off the autopilot and bring heart, mind, and soul back into everything you do. So the next time you need to make a decision, instead of doing what comes automatically, spend some time thinking about alternatives, even options that don't come naturally to you. Turn it around, and turn yourself around. It's challenging to defy gravity, but you give yourself a fresh infusion of energy.

Explore new directions, and get out of your rut. Remember, staying in a rut is a choice, like everything else in life. If you feel enthusiastic or happy about something or someone, let it lead you to a deeper understanding of yourself and a greater joy in being alive. Stop blocking your energy. If you feel the urge to express yourself on a canvas, if you feel like dancing, running, making love, laughing, give yourself permission to adore life, and give yourself up to the passion of the joyful activity.

And finally in your voyage of self-discovery, make sure you stop clinging to habits and mindsets that don't express who you are anymore. Stop clinging to them, however comfortable they may feel, because you don't want to exert the energy needed to change them. Try thinking of old, outdated thoughts and actions as old tea leaves: once they've been used, it's time to throw them out.

*Each cup of tea represents an imaginary voyage.*
—Catherine Donzel, contemporary French writer

## A Shared Life

One of the guiding principles of the Japanese tea ceremony is to give guests every consideration. Putting your heart into everything you do includes the way you interact with others. Are you putting your heart into your relationships? Are your relationships meaningful?

# Tea Time

It isn't just the Chinese and Japanese who make tea drinking a special occasion. Wherever it is drunk, tea has developed its own rituals. It may not be the drink of passion, but it is the drink of conversation.

In Russia, the strong tea of the samovar is soothed with a lump of sugar and jam. In France, the custom has grown of drinking tea in a languid fashion with afternoon pastries. In Egypt, tea comes in a glass on a metal tray with some water and sugar. In many Arab countries, tea is the drink of friendship and is always drunk with sweet pastries.

In England, the ritual of afternoon tea all started with Anna, the Duchess of Bedford, in the eighteenth century. Back then, the English ate only two meals a day—breakfast in the early morning and a huge dinner at night. In between, they simply starved. What the duchess did was to invite friends in the afternoon for a meal at five o'clock in her rooms at Belvoir Castle. The menu included small cakes, bread-and-butter sandwiches, sweets, and, of course, tea.

The practice of inviting friends for afternoon tea was soon picked up by other social hostesses in London. A pot of tea was brewed and served in fine porcelain. The snacks were then passed among the guests, the main purpose of the visit being conversation.

What the English discovered, the Chinese have also been practicing for centuries. Writer Lin Yutang quotes an old proverb in his book, *The Wisdom of China:* "When the tea is well brewed and the incense has a pure fragrance, it's a delight if friends drop in."

While afternoon tea is not of the same spiritual nature as the Chinese or Japanese tea ceremonies, there is something very calming and meditative about it in its ritualized service and comforting foods. As Henry James said in his novel *The Portrait of a Lady,* "There are few hours in life more agreeable than the hour dedicated to the ceremony known as afternoon tea."

The first tea shop opened in London in 1884 and belonged to the ABC Bakery. It was soon followed by others. Then came the afternoon, or tea, dance, where single ladies could always find a partner to twirl them to the music playing. Today the cup of tea is still fundamental at royal parties, cricket matches, and church fund-raisers.

Trend forecasters believe that tea bars serving tea and alcohol in cocktails, such as Earl Grey "mar-tea-nis," and tea temples to help you unwind with tea rituals may take over the coffee shops' reign in the United States. Soon tea breaks will mean so much more than waiting for a kettle to boil.

Most of what makes life meaningful and wonderful grows out of our connectedness to others, but relationships can also be a source of confusion and complexity. It's easy to get lost in relationships and forget who you are, but the truer you are to yourself in relationships and the more you put into them, the more helpful, meaningful, and delicious they can become.

Begin once again with self-assessment. What kind of person are you, and are you true to yourself within relationships? Ask yourself a few fundamental questions:

Do I like to be around people (extrovert), or do I feel drained by others (introvert)?

What do I value or respect most in other people?

What relationships in my past have contributed most to my happiness?

What relationships in the past have detracted from my happiness?

Remember that your answers to these questions will change through time as your needs and circumstances change. Relationships—who, what kind, and when—are as much a process as personal growth. What worked a few years ago may be wrong for you now. Your understanding of what matters will refine and change as, over years, you discover the effects of particular relationship patterns.

Now that you have taken stock of your current attitude toward relationships, think about all the people who figure most in your life right now. Be as honest as you can as you ask yourself these questions:

Are there areas of tension in my current relationships?
Do particular groups of people fill me with dread?
Do I feel put upon, put down, or put out by a given relation-ship or relationships in general?

For every *yes,* elaborate with who, what, where, when, how, and why. Then prepare for change. Remember, as you move forward equipped with self-knowledge and conscious of areas of your rela-tionship life that you want to change, that any change in relation-ships affects at least two people. Every change you make will call forth a response, not just in you but also in the other person.

A few responses to change are predictable. Resistance from others is a sure thing. Change is always threatening to other people, as it means we become less predictable, less understandable, and less famil-iar. You can ease the way for others by keeping in mind how it looks from the other person's point of view and finding ways to inform and reassure them. Give your close connections time to get used to the new you. Tell them they have nothing to fear, and let them know that the changes you are making are not about you loving or liking them less but about knowing and caring for yourself better, which can only be a mutual gain for both. Tell others what you are up to and how you are moving in the direction you need and want to go. Show them how much happier you feel, and let them know their feelings are important to you because you want them to be happy too. Share your journey of self-discovery. You have to begin with yourself, but you can't travel alone. The other people in your life will want to be included.

Okay, let's say you have begun to assess where you are in relation to others and kept others informed of your intention to change. It still remains to put yourself and your intentions into action. Each kind of relationship has unique challenges, and you need to plan ahead for those challenges. Then take steps to recharge your relationships with others to suit the kind of life you want.

For family and loved ones, build an atmosphere of trust, collaboration, and communication by calling regular meetings in which common goals are discussed, plans are made together, and problems are shared. You could declare one day a week a family recharge day, where you give yourself and each other time to do something completely out of the ordinary or nothing at all. You could allow yourself and others time and space alone, to pursue other relationships and activities outside the family as well.

When it comes to friendships, know your limits. You can't be everyone's friend. Friendships can be one of the richest gifts in life, but they can also weigh us down with confusion when we fail to set realistic boundaries. Every friendship represents a commitment of time and attention, and each one of us has only so much time and attention, so start slowly and think about the level of a new friendship as much as you would about a job. Practice "less is more," making the most of the time you have together with plenty of breathing room between. Be honest when you don't have the time or give friends times that are off limits.

We teach people how to be our friends, children, parents, partners, neighbors, and coworkers. If we know ourselves and respect

# Japanese Tea Ceremony

A Japanese cup of tea is more than is implied by the name for the ceremony—*cha no yu* ("hot water for tea"). It is, in fact, a quiet interlude during which host and guests strive for spiritual refreshment and harmony with the universe. The Japanese tea ceremony captures all the elements of Japanese philosophy and artistic beauty and interweaves four principles—harmony (with people and nature), respect (for others), purity (of heart and mind), and tranquility. It grew from the custom of Zen Buddhist monks drinking tea from a single bronze bowl in front of a statue of their founder, Bodhidharma, during their act of worship. Over the centuries, rituals gradually developed around the religious significance and the use and appreciation of the utensils needed for preparing and serving tea.

Today, the ceremony may be performed in a specially designed room in a private house, in a teahouse within a private garden, in a designated complex of rooms in the workplace, or in a public teahouse.

A full tea, or *Chaji,* involves a meal and the serving of two different types of tea and can last for four hours, but shorter, simpler teas can be served to suit individual occasions. Ceremonies are held to honor special guests, to celebrate particular occasions such as the blossoming of the cherry trees in spring, to admire the full moon, or simply to gather together a few friends. For each occasion, the flowers, vase, wall hangings, and tea wares are chosen carefully to suit the event, the time of year, and the desired atmosphere.

When the guests arrive, they are not greeted at the door by their host or hostess but are guided through a series of open doors to a waiting room. Here they are served a small porcelain cup of hot water taken from a kettle in the tearoom as a foretaste of the water to be used in the tea making. They then make their way quietly and calmly into the garden and are met halfway at a gate by the host or hostess, who opens the gate and silently greets them with a bow. This gentle passage through the garden represents a breaking of ties with the everyday world and allows a clarifying of the senses through the enjoyment of the sweet sound of trickling water and birdsong, and the visual pleasure of trees, plants, and blossoms. Nearby stands a stone lantern to light the path when evening falls. The guests pause to cleanse their hands and mouth with water from a stone basin of running water. The entrance to the tea room is so low that everyone must stoop to go through—a symbolic gesture of humility—and once inside, guests spend a few minutes admiring the kettle, the scrolls decorating the walls, and the flowers. They then kneel on mats, sit back on their heels, and watch while their host performs the ceremony of the lighting of the charcoal fire. A meal of fine foods is then served, but although this can last for more than an hour, it is not the main event but merely a preparation of the body for the tea ceremony, which is to come. After eating, the guests step back outside into the garden while the tearoom is freshened for the tea-brewing ceremony. They then return inside and spend the next forty-five minutes sharing a bowl of thick tea prepared by whisking powdered green tea (*matcha*) into hot water with a bamboo whisk. A sweetcake made with bean curd is served and is eaten with little wooden picks that each guest has brought to the ceremony.

By this time, the fire has burned low, and the host or hostess performs a different fire-lighting ceremony and waits, while conversation continues, for the kettle to boil for a second time. Individual bowls of thin watery tea are then prepared and served to each guest in turn, again accompanied by little dainty sweets. Once this is over, final greetings are exchanged, and everyone leaves.

Because the tea ceremony involves an understanding and appreciation of a complex combination of sensual and spiritual elements and the ceremony involves almost every aspect of Japanese life—architecture, history, food, craft, art-the training to become a tea master is long and demands complete commitment. A student must bring to his or her training all the knowledge and skills learned and developed in everyday life as well as human qualities such as sensitivity, awareness, skills of communication. It's possible to learn enough of the basic rituals to create a tea after three years or so of dedicated study, but becoming a true tea master is a lifetime's work, and the training process is never really completed.

ourselves, we have the ability to show others how best we can relate. We can dump the extra baggage of expectations that we have allowed others to associate with us. We can build new habits to enhance good relationships and repair broken ones. We may find that some people and their needs don't fit our lives. We're bogged down because we keep taking on new people the way we do groceries.

Give those who share your life every consideration, but make sure you give yourself every consideration too. Relationships are a gift, but never forget that the more you learn to respect and be true to yourself, the more honest and satisfying your relationships will become.

> *He boils milk with fresh ginger, a quarter of a vanilla bean, and tea that is so dark and fine-leaved that it looks like black dust. He strains it and puts cane sugar in both our cups. There's something euphorically invigorating and yet filling about it. It tastes the way I imagine the Far East must taste.*
> —Peter Hoeg, *Smilla's Sense of Snow*

## You Are So Much More

We spend our lives looking for meaning and happiness in the material world, believing this is our only reality. We search for fulfillment in external things like money, career, food, sex, clothes, and so on, but this approach never works. Something is always missing.

Of course you live in the material world and you have wants and needs, but you are also so much more. When you find yourself saying, "There must be more to life than this," you are right: what you see with your eyes is not all that you get. There is another path, which leads to a strong sense of inner awareness, trust, creativity, and intuition, and this is where you discover peace and serenity and truth.

Think of all those times in your life when you have been lifted beyond thoughts and feelings to something more: perhaps you were holding a newborn baby, listening to music, falling in love, or running in the sand. These are the times when you become aware of your own spiritual energy and connection to the universe, and these are the times when you really begin to understand yourself, your relationships, and your life.

It doesn't matter whether you believe in God or are more comfortable with other terms such as higher power, inner guidance, or higher self. Your sense of spirituality does not depend on spiritual beliefs; your spirituality, which is your ultimate truth, lies in you, and you know it every time you rise above the material. So whenever you can, suspend disbelief. Let yourself be taken on a wonderful spiritual journey of amazing self-discovery, and awaken to your own brilliance of being.

## Keep Moving Forward

Once you start the adventure of self-discovery, you begin the journey to a deeper, richer, more spiritual life that reflects who you are and what is best and most important in and to you. Just like a tea ceremony effortlessly performed, it all looks simple, but the simplicity belies the difficulty of following the guidelines strictly. There will be setbacks and moments of confusion, and you won't get there overnight—it's going to take a while—but all you need to do is keep moving in the right direction, by beginning each day being true to who you are and putting your heart into everything you do.

*[I am] a hardened and shameless tea drinker, who for twenty years diluted his meals with only the infusion of the fascinating plant; who with tea amused the evening, with tea solaced the midnight, and with tea welcomed the morning.*
—Samuel Johnson (1709–1784), English writer

# Nourishing Blend № 8

## *healing with tea*

**About Tea:** Tea that is made the right way, and is not too strong or too weak, has a healing energy. It can keep your body healthy and refresh your spirit.

**About Life:** You can heal your life.

Modern medical research has shown that tea provides a number of wonderful health benefits. Drinking three to four cups of mild, good-quality tea each day can boost immunity and mood and provide protection from all kinds of ailments. Why not open your heart and your mind and let the soothing energy of tea bring healing into your life?

## Healing with Tea

Possibly the most important thing about tea is its ability to relax the drinker. When freshly brewed tea is poured from the teapot, it is normally too hot to drink. This is a wonderful opportunity to sit back, relax, watch the steam rise from your cup, and allow the aroma to fill your nostrils. Tea is a silent but powerful healing influence in our lives. As you wait for the tea to cool down and experience the pleasure of the moment, tensions slip away.

Wouldn't it be amazing if you could carry that healing, relaxing state of mind around all the time? Well, you can, if you can learn how to let go of three things: your past, your guilt, and your fear.

## Let go of the past

Do you recognize any of the following thoughts?

"If only I had done that."
"I wish I had said something else."
"Why did I do that?"
"If only I could do it again!"

We've all been there—worrying about things, blaming ourselves for what happened, and wishing we had done something differently.

We can all look back and regret, but we cannot change the past; if we continue to agonize over what we should and shouldn't have done, our lives will become miserable. You can't change what you said or did, so let the past go. Understand your past, but don't use it as an excuse not to move forward. If you did wrong or messed up, apologize and try to make amends. Stop blaming yourself all the time. Nobody is perfect. We all make mistakes. Learn from your mistakes, accept responsibility, understand what went wrong, and use the experience and knowledge you have gained to make positive changes and move forward with optimism.

If you constantly dwell on the past, you are sure to feel unhappy and unfulfilled. The past is there to be understood, not dwelled on. Let it go. Start right now. Stop making excuses, leave the past behind, and take action in the present.

## Leave guilt to the martyrs

Guilt drags you back into the past and does nothing to help your present. Guilt destroys happiness. It burns your self-confidence like overly steeped tea burns your throat. Many of us are so wracked with guilt we fly from pillar to post trying to be all things to everybody. Guilt drives us always toward a no-win situation, with our chances of happiness getting smaller and smaller.

If this is you, stop for a moment. Why are you choosing to be a victim? Why is guilt souring your life? Guilt will burn you up unless you get rid of it, so make the decision to kick it out of your life. There are no half-measures here. You cannot decide to let it come in now and again. Imagine your guilt floating away in a bubble or like a balloon in the air. Watch it vanish into the skies, and then don't think about it again.

## Let go of fear

Many of us aren't as happy or as fulfilled as we could be because fear holds us back. We are frightened of rejection, of making mistakes, of the unknown, of challenging ourselves, or of looking silly. Often, though, when we feel fear what we are really experiencing is laziness. Most of us deep down believe that life should be easy, and we complain when it isn't. How often have you thought, "Why me?" "This isn't fair!" "I shouldn't have to do this." It's as if we expect our lives to be problem free, but the problem-free life is about as invigorating as a tea that is far too weak and has no flavor.

Whoever said that life was supposed to be easy? It isn't. If we could all accept this, we could move on to solving the challenges life throws at us rather than complaining about them. It is only in meeting and solving challenges that our life has meaning. Challenges require us to be creative, hardworking, skillful, brave, and clever. Confronting challenges helps us to grow spiritually, emotionally, physically, and mentally.

When psychologist Mihaly Csikszentmihalyi completed his studies on flow and optimal experience, he summarized his findings by saying, "Every day, the happy person does at least one difficult thing." In other words, instead of avoiding challenges, we should welcome them. This isn't to say you should deliberately seek out difficulties—a balanced life is one in which you are fully engaged, not overwhelmed—but if the difficulty is in fact a lesson we need to learn, the best course of action is to embrace the lesson, face the difficulty, and move forward.

Most of us can't take this step, and we do all we can to avoid challenges rather than face them. We hesitate, make excuses, ignore, forget, and hope they will go away, or we deaden ourselves to the pain through addiction or pleasure seeking. Trouble is, when we don't face our fears, we stop growing as human beings. We become bitter and stuck. Our spirit withers.

As hard as it may seem to accept, problems, pain, and suffering are a part of life. They give life its full-bodied flavor, and without them life would be bland and tasteless. We all need to find the courage to let fear go, face our problems, however tough, deal with them if we can, learn from them, and move on. This is the only way to lead a rich and full life.

Now and again you may find that regret, fear, and guilt bubble to the surface. Don't let them get a foothold anymore; the only reward you will get is feeling bad about yourself. Remember that guilt, fear, and regret achieve absolutely nothing. You may think you are doing a lot when you feel guilty or worry, but you aren't helping anyone or changing anything. Keep practicing letting go of guilt, fear, and regret and moving forward, and you'll find it gets easier and easier to heal yourself and to live.

*I hope next time when we meet, we won't be fighting each other. Instead we will be drinking tea together.*
—Jackie Chan, *Rumble in the Bronx*

# Healing Power of Tea

Drinking tea is good for you. The humble cuppa contains a wealth of nutrients, such as vitamin C, flavonoids, and polyphenols, which have been found to help boost the body's defenses against serious illness. Green and black teas are rich in natural antioxidants, which fight the damaging effects of free radicals caused by pollution, smoking, and sunlight. They also contain vitamin B6, which plays a key role in the body's metabolism, and vitamins B1 and B2, essential for releasing energy from food and normal thyroid function.

Tea is also rich in two key minerals—manganese, which is essential for bone growth and body development; and potassium, which helps keep the heart beating and maintain the fluid levels in the body. Tea is also tooth friendly, as it is one of the few sources of fluoride. Oral hygienists increasingly believe that tea improves overall oral health by preventing tooth decay and reducing plaque.

Scientists have revealed that black and green teas appear to help protect people against Alzheimer's disease by altering brain chemistry, and have recently published their findings in the academic journal for herbal medicine *Phytotherapy Research*. There is also growing scientific evidence that the antioxidant effects of the flavonoids in tea are important for helping to prevent cancer of such organs as the pancreas, prostate, colon, esophagus, and mouth. For example, a recent study reported in the respected medical journal the *Lancet* found that chemicals in green tea appear to be effective at preventing and treating cancer. "Green tea offers several advantages as anti-cancer products because it is non-toxic, produces few side effects, is widely available and cheap," wrote Canadian scientists Denis Gingras and Richard Beliveau in the *Lancet*. Other researchers from the University of California have found that prostate cancer cells grow more slowly in men who regularly drink green or black tea.

Of equal importance is tea's ability to combat heart disease and reduce the risk of strokes; studies show that tea reduces blood cholesterol and blood clotting and lowers blood pressure. Perhaps the most striking

*continued*

development in medical research has been the recent review by researchers at Harvard Medical School. It was found that a person who drinks a single cup of tea a day can cut the risk of having a heart attack by up to 44 percent. This is because the powerful antioxidants in tea counteract fatty deposits in the arteries. To sum up, a good-quality tea can help keep cholesterol down and improve circulation by helping to increase blood flow and prevent hardening of the arteries.

The evidence for the healing power of tea is overwhelming, but as with everything, too much can bring on negative side effects, such as digestive upsets, insomnia, headaches, and stained teeth. Such symptoms are not only associated with high volumes of intake—more than six cups a day—but also with particularly strong brews of tea. Generally, any side effects can be easily mitigated by cutting down to three or four cups a day and drinking lightly brewed tea.

*If you are cold, tea will warm you; if you are too heated, it will cool you; if you are depressed, it will cheer you; if you are excited, it will calm you.*
—Anonymous

## Healing Yourself

Self-healing, the desire to be whole again and to be comfortable with yourself, can really begin only when you start letting go of all those feelings and thoughts, like guilt, fear, and regret, that make you feel bad about yourself and your life. Once you've let go of them, you'll feel light and free and ready to make good choices for yourself.

From now on, become your own best friend. Take care of yourself. Don't stress yourself with negative thoughts about yourself.

# Tea Therapy

Here is a guide to the scientifically proved health benefits of some of the most popular teas:

### Standard black tea: Protects against heart disease
Packed with antioxidant polyphenols to destroy harmful free radicals and boost your body's resistance to infection, black tea also has about half the caffeine of fresh coffee. Drinking three or four cuppas daily can help protect against disease and aging. The drink is even thought to help safeguard artery walls from damage—just two cups a day appear to reduce the risk of high cholesterol and heart disease. Cataracts and tooth decay are other ailments against which tea is thought to be effective. The downside is that black tea also contains caffeine and tannins. Caffeine can increase heart rate and trigger headaches, and tannins can inhibit your absorption of iron and protein, so try not to drink in excess (more than four lightly brewed cups a day), and leave half an hour between tea drinking and eating meals.

### Earl Grey: Good digestive aid
The bergamot oil with which Earl Grey is flavored comes from a type of orange that is thought to help digestion because it stimulates production of stomach enzymes, helping to break down food. This tea may be most beneficial, therefore, if it is drunk after a meal.

### Green tea: Immune boosting
Because green tea is rolled and dried rather than fermented, like black tea is, it retains more nutrients and has a higher antioxidant—immune-boosting, antiaging—effect. It also contains less tannin and caffeine than black tea. Research has found that green tea can help prevent a whole range of diseases, including diabetes and cancer of the stomach, prostate, and lungs. It can also help reduce cholesterol levels and appears to give more effective protection against Alzheimer's than black tea.

Finally, drinking four cups of green tea (without milk) a day is thought to help you lose weight. Studies at the American Society for Clinical Nutrition found that one of the compounds in green tea, catechol, increases metabolism and reduces the amount of fat your body absorbs by as much as 30 percent.

### Pu-erh tea: Refreshing and energizing
Pu-erh tea is thought to help lower cholesterol, balance blood sugar, clear the mind, and aid digestion. It's an ideal health drink for young and old.

### Redbush tea: Great skin
Made from a South African tea bush, redbush, or *rooibos,* is one of the healthiest teas around. It is the only naturally caffeine-free black tea and contains half the amount of tannin—which can inhibit the absorption of iron and protein—as standard tea. It has a slightly sweet, perfumed flavor and can be served with milk or lemon. It is richer in antioxidants than black tea, can help promote healthy skin and ease eczema, and can help prevent diseases including cancer. It has also been used to calm the symptoms of irritable bowel syndrome and reduce muscle cramps, and it has anti-inflammatory properties.

### White tea: Reducing cancer risk
Whereas black tea is made from tea leaves, white tea is made from only the buds of the tea bush. This gives it even greater health benefits than green tea. It tastes like a slightly milder version of black tea and can be drunk with or without milk.

### Decaffeinated tea
A cup of decaffeinated tea contains only 2 mg of caffeine, whereas a standard cup contains around 40 mg. Decaffeinated tea is good for those who are sensitive to caffeine, such as migraine sufferers and pregnant women. Pregnant women are advised to limit their caffeine consumption to 300 mg a day, because excessive amounts have been linked to low-birth-weight babies and even miscarriage. Critics fear that the chemicals found in the decaffeination process not only strip tea of nutrients, so it's not as

*continued*

good for you as regular tea, but also taint the tea, but the FSA (Food Sta
Standards Agency) says none are cause for concern. Some organic brands
use carbon dioxide rather than chemicals to remove the caffeine.

### Lemon tea: Energizing

Lemon tea is mainly sugar with tea solids, and therefore it contains more
calories than ordinary tea. Although there is no actual lemon in it, it does
contain small quantities of antioxidants, in particular, added vitamin C.
Each cup contains the equivalent amount of vitamin C found in a Satsuma
orange.

### Iced tea: Cooling, soothing, and refreshing

This ready-made, fruit-infused drink has a refreshing flavor and consists
of water, sugar, and tea solids, which means it is higher in calories than
standard tea. However it still contains those vital antioxidants, and unlike
most soft drinks, it is free from artificial colorings and flavorings.

### Fruit teas: Good alternative to soft drinks

Fruit teas do not typically have the antioxidant or mineral properties of
black or green teas, and researchers have found that they are acidic, and
many contribute to dental problems. They are, however, caffeine free and
lower in sugar than most soft drinks.

### Herbal teas: Healing and soothing

Herbal teas have a wide range of health benefits. Mint tea, for example,
stimulates production of digestive juices and can ease the discomfort of
irritable bowel syndrome and aid digestion. Clean-tasting chamomile tea
can help soothe the nerves and relax the muscles, so is a good nighttime
drink. Elderflower tea is said to help alleviate symptoms of allergies and
is often recommended to people with hay fever. Herbal teas are caffeine
free. For best results, make them in a pot because otherwise oils from the
leaves evaporate in the steam. Herbal teas that contain medicinal compounds such as ginseng or St. John's wort should be treated with the same
caution as herbal medicines because they can interfere with some con-

ventional drugs. Always check with your pharmacist or doctor before self-prescribing.

### Peppermint tea: Digestion
As with all herbal tisanes, peppermint tea is caffeine free. Studies have shown it has an antispasmodic effect on the digestive system, so it's ideal for relieving the symptoms of irritable bowel syndrome, bloating, and indigestion. It's the perfect after-dinner treat.

### Chamomile tea: Calming and soothing
Great for relieving anxiety and insomnia, chamomile tea, like peppermint, has an antispasmodic effect so can be taken to ease stomach cramps. Its calming effect is provided by valerianic acid. Drinking German chamomile and applying the cooled tea to your face can help acne. For maximum health benefits, make your own infusion with dried flowers, or look for teas produced entirely from chamomile flowers, as they will have more nutrients.

### Ginger tea: Beating nausea
Ginger tea is an excellent tonic for morning or travel sickness as well as for improving sluggish circulation. It's also great for your immune system, helping to ward off colds and sore throats. Making your own ginger tea will provide the most health benefits. Boil thick slices of ginger root in water, strain, and add lemon or honey to taste.

### Raspberry leaf tea: For late pregnancy and menstrual irregularity
Raspberry leaf tea can tone the muscles of the uterus to promote shorter, smoother labor. Also contains calcium, iron, B vitamins, and magnesium. Mothers-to-be can drink the tea at about thirty-four weeks *but not before* because of the leaf's stimulating effect on the uterus. Drink one or two cups a day (always consult a doctor if you are pregnant or hoping to get pregnant). Can also be helpful for regulating irregular menstrual cycles and easing PMS and heavy periods.

Don't disparage yourself—that's no way to treat your best friend. Try some of these healing exercises:

- Start each day with a short prayer of thanks, and end each day with the same.
- Become your own best friend whenever you are tempted to criticize yourself or when your self-esteem is low. Imagine you have stepped out of your body and that you are standing next to yourself. Now look at yourself. What would you say that was comforting and helpful? How would you encourage you to be more confident? What would you say to your best friend? Perhaps you would put your arm around her and tell her she is doing really well and that you appreciate all her good qualities. Talk to yourself the way you would to your best friend. The technique is so simple and so effective. Become your own best friend, and your self-esteem will immediately increase.
- Write down five positive things about each day. If it's hard to think of any, remember that the sun came out, a flower opened, a bird sang, someone smiled at you, or you heard a song on the radio you enjoyed. Happiness often resides in these little things.
- Set positive boundaries, and dare to say no.
- Always speak positively about yourself, and don't put yourself down.
- Cherish your dreams. If they seem impossible, trust they will come to you in the right way, in the right time, and in the right place.
- Remember you are a human being, not a human doing.
- Eat right, and get some exercise every day.
- Surround yourself with positive people and uplifting things. Read and look to that which boosts you. Choose your friends with care. Listen to beautiful and peaceful music.

- Smile! And do it often.
- Visualize yourself as healthy and happy.
- Read spiritual books.
- Do you want to receive? Start with giving, and give with a heart full of joy. Enjoy yourself in the giving itself. It doesn't have to be material giving. It can also be immaterial things such as kindness, love, a smile, a word of sympathy.
- Practice forgiveness. Everyone makes mistakes.
- Treat yourself as you want to be treated.
- Be fair and honest.
- Don't act; just be yourself.
- If life gets really tough and you can't see a way forward, keep in mind that it will not be like this forever and after the darkest night the sun will shine again.
- Enjoy nature.
- Regularly take time to see what is living in your heart. Try to express it. If you can't speak it, you can try to write it or start a diary or do something creative. Find something that appeals to you, such as drawing, flower arranging, or dancing. Art, creativity, is a great way to heal yourself because you can pour your feelings and emotions into it. It's fun too. Don't say, "I'm not talented." You can try. You can learn. Just start for your own pleasure. In this way you can express your feelings, and this is very important in the process of healing yourself.
- Take time out for a cuppa. Experiment until you find teas that suit every mood and occasion.

*You can taste and feel, but not describe, the exquisite state of repose produced by tea, that precious drink, which drives away the five causes of sorrow.*
—Ch'ien Lung (1710–1789), Chinese emperor

# Making Herbal Teas

Tea made from fresh-picked herbs tastes wonderful. However, many herbs may not be available fresh, either because of the season or their growing environment. A perfect cup of tea can still be brewed with quality dried herbs.

When making herbal tea, it is important to use a glass, porcelain, or glazed earthenware pot for brewing, because some metals can react with the herbs. Always warm the container to prevent the tea from cooling off too quickly and also to prevent the container from breaking. Many types of strainers and tea balls are available, but the simplest is a fine-mesh stainless steel gravy strainer found in kitchen stores. This method allows the herbs to float and move around during brewing. If you prefer a tea ball, use a large one.

Because herbal teas can be brewed from leaves, roots, bark, seeds, or flowers, alone or in combination, bear in mind the following brewing techniques:

- Teas made from the leaves or flowers are infused to protect the more delicate oils from evaporating. To make an infusion, place the herbs in the warmed teapot or canning jar, pour gently boiling water over the herbs, cover to prevent evaporation, steep for 10 to 15 minutes, and strain. In general, use 1 teaspoon of dried or 3 teaspoons of fresh, bruised herb per cup of water.
- Teas made from the roots, bark, or seeds are *decocted* to release their properties. A decoction requires the roots or bark to be cut into small pieces and the seeds to be bruised with a mortar and pestle or the back of a spoon. Place $1/2$ to 1 ounce of herb into a pot with 1 pint (2 cups) of cold water, bring to a gentle boil, reduce heat, simmer gently for 10 to 20 minutes, and strain. Teas made with stronger spices such as ginger, clove, or cinnamon will need to be adjusted for personal tastes.
- To make a tea with both roots/bark/seeds and leaves/flowers, follow the directions for making a decoction using just the roots,

bark, or seeds. Pour the strained decoction over the leaves or flowers, and infuse as above.

- Herbal iced teas follow the same procedures as above but should be brewed double strength. After straining, chill for 30 minutes, and pour over a glass full of ice.
- Most herbal teas don't need sweetening, but sugar or, preferably, local honey can be added. Unused tea should be refrigerated and used within 24 hours of brewing. One final tip: store all your herbs, roots, seeds, flowers, or leaves in dark, glass containers. Place the containers in a dark place. The teas will stay fresher longer.

## Let Yourself Be Happy

With so many opportunities to heal ourselves, why are we so unhappy? Happiness is a natural part of the human condition; we only need to believe this and then allow ourselves to feel it.

You deserve to be happy. Make happiness your number one goal. Appreciate the joys in life. Be grateful for the simple pleasures. Wherever possible, replace "I've got to" with "I'd be happy to." Feel free to be your most joyous self: enthusiastic, kind, generous, forgiving, and loving. The more you let joy into your life, the more you love; and the more you love, the better you will feel.

# Herbal Tea Remedies

Here are some herbal tea recipes for you to try. They cover a range of remedies for everyday living.

**Angelica tea** is a remedy for colds, coughs, pleurisy, flatulence, rheumatism, fever, nervousness, poor skin, appetite loss, and indigestion and can also be used as a blood tonic. Fresh angelica root stimulates the production of digestive juices and improves the flow of bile. This tea resembles china tea with a celery taste.

To 1 teaspoonful of dried or 3 teaspoons of fresh, add 1 cup of boiling water. Steep to taste.

**Chamomile tea** has soothing, calming, and relaxing properties. It helps digestion, coughs, colds, and poor skin, and is used as a liver tonic. The entire chamomile plant can be used for tea. However, the flowers are the most flavorful.

To 2 teaspoons dried flowers or 1 tablespoon of fresh flowers, add 1 cup boiling water. Steep to taste.

**Dill tea** helps an upset stomach, indigestion, coughs, colds, and bronchitis, fever, sore throat, and tendency to infection, urinary tract infections, and sleep disorders. It stimulates the appetite, acts as a nerve sedative, and is a blood and liver tonic. Dill seeds have been proven the most effective.

Crush the seeds or use a grinder. To 1 teaspoonful of crushed seeds, add 1 cup of boiling water. Steep to taste.

**Fennel tea** helps bronchitis, digestive problems, and coughs; stimulates movement of food through the stomach and intestines, dries respiratory phlegm, and destroys germs. It makes a good after-dinner tea.

Use crushed or ground seeds. To 1 or $1^{1}/_{2}$ teaspoons of ground seeds, add 1 cup of boiling water. Steep to taste.

**Lemon balm tea** will perk you up in the morning and will help bloating, gas, mood disorders, bronchial inflammation, high blood pressure, mild vomiting, toothache, earache, and headaches. Lemon balm has antibacterial and antiviral properties.

Use the plant's leaves. A good combination is lemon balm and fennel. To 1 teaspoon of crushed lemon balm, add 1 cup boiling water. Steep 10 minutes. Take twice a day.

**Peppermint tea** helps indigestion, head colds, headaches, appetite loss, bronchitis, fever, and gall bladder problems. It can be used as a blood and liver tonic.

To 1 teaspoon of peppermint, add $1/2$ cup of boiling water. Steep 10 minutes.

**Thyme tea** helps bronchitis, coughs, sinuses, nose and throat, larynx, and whooping cough. It can be used as an antibacterial. Thyme tea aids digestion.

To $1^1/_2$ teaspoons thyme, add 1 cup boiling water. Steep 10 minutes. Take several times a day, but do not exceed 3 cups per day.

**Ginger tea** helps appetite loss, motion sickness, upset stomach; relieves gas; loosens phlegm; and soothes earaches.

To 1 teaspoon of ginger, add 1 cup boiling water. Steep 5 minutes.

# Two Soothing Tea Recipes

**Take-It-Easy Blend**
This combination of herbs is created especially for relief after a stressful day. You'll need:

$^1/_4$ cup dried spearmint
$^1/_4$ cup dried lemongrass
1 cup dried lemon balm
$^1/_2$ cup dried catnip
$^3/_4$ cup dried chamomile flowers

Blend all herbs thoroughly, and store in an airtight container away from heat and light. To make tea, use 2 teaspoons of blend for each cup of boiling water.

**Calming Spirit Tea Blend**
This very tasty tea is wonderful iced or hot. These herbs are traditionally used to calm the nerves, settle the stomach, and uplift. Other herbs can be added as desired. You'll need:

1 cup dried rosemary leaves
1 cup dried lavender flowers
1 cup dried spearmint
$^1/_2$ cup dried chamomile
$^1/_4$ to $^1/_2$ cup dried cloves

Blend all herbs thoroughly, and store in an airtight container away from heat and light. To make tea, use one teaspoon of loose herbs per cup of water. You can prepare the tea in a tea ball, or mix the loose herbs with water in a teapot and then strain tea into a cup. Or you could place a handful of herbs in a muslin bag and add the bag to your bathwater for a soothing treat.

# Nourishing Blend № 9
## *meditate with tea*

**About Tea:** You can combine the pure bliss of tea with the power of meditation to maximize the therapeutic benefits of tea long after it has been consumed.

**About Life:** Allow tea to help you find your path to inner peace.

If you have a cup of tea in your hand, what else can you do but sit down and take a break? There are few more relaxing and refreshing things in life than a soothing cup of tea and a break. Meditation with tea is quite literally fuel for body and mind and spirit.

*Inhale the sweet smell emanating from the tea as the hot water liberates its essence. Feel a growing sense of relaxation as the mind focus is drawn to the rhythmic movements of breath. Inhale the vital energy life force. Exhale the energy of union with the universe. Allow yourself to fall gently into deep concentration on the space just following the exhale. Deeper and deeper the Universe expands, moving through translucent space that shimmers like a black pearl. In this moment, tea is brought to your lips by a slow steady hand. A taste bittersweet as life itself.*
—James Burnett, environmentalist, president of Ecology Works

## Combining Meditation with Tea

A cup of tea is meditation.

Meditation is a time to find peace—to daydream, relax, let your mind wander, and return with fresh insights—or to focus all your attention on one activity or word. That's exactly what you do when you make and serve tea. When you drink tea, there is peace. The simple act of making tea requires you to pay attention. You cannot rush the procedure. Too little time, and it will taste bland. Too much time, and it will taste bitter. You can't drink it quickly, either. It needs to be enjoyed at your leisure, giving you time to reflect, imagine, and dream.

Meditation is the gift you can give to yourself of quiet, uninterrupted time. You relax your body, release tension, and calm your mind and by so doing gain better control over your thoughts and your life. For millions of people for centuries, mindful preparation of tea and drinking it with intent has been a form of meditation that brings positive results for mind, body, and spirit.

*The best state of mind in which to drink tea is one of deep meditation. The second best is while looking at a beautiful landscape or listening to music. The third best is during stimulating conversation. In all cases it is necessary to aspire towards a quiet and tranquil frame of mind.*
—Paichang (729–814), Chinese Ch'an (Zen) master

*The first cup of tea makes the mouth and throat glisten; the second brings all worries to an end; the third cup brings comfort to dry intestines and even if surrounded by thousands of books you can absorb yourself in studying a single topic without distractions; the fourth produces a light sweat which expels all complaints of the mind through the pores of the skin; the fifth*

*cup cleanses both the flesh and bones; the sixth cup is akin to penetrating the meaning of the immortal spirit; after the seventh cup you can drink no more. From the armpits a fresh breeze gently rises, you start to wonder where Mount Ponglae is, and Yodong wishes to ride the fresh breeze and fly away.*
—Lu T'ung (733–804), Tang Dynasty poet

## Begin the Journey to Inner Peace

Tea quenches your thirst, but it does something bigger: it refreshes your spirit as well. If you've ever relaxed with a cup of tea and let your mind wander, then you already know how to meditate with tea. You just need a few guidelines to help you get the best out of the experience. So next time you put the kettle on, begin your journey to inner peace with the following suggestions.

### Meditating with tea: Guidelines for beginners

Quiet is essential for meditation. Some people have the ability to find inner peace when noise is all around them, but if you are a beginner the silence of stillness is important. Find a place at home where you can be alone and quiet. You may at first feel a little anxious being alone, believing it to be associated with loneliness. It is not.

To encourage the right frame of mind, start by making yourself comfortable. Take off your shoes and belt or anything tight, and sit or kneel or lie down. Do make sure your back is supported. Close your eyes, and empty your mind as you would empty a dishwasher or a trash can. Now start to sense what is going on around you. What do you hear, smell, and feel?

Make sure your spine is straight (whether sitting or lying down), and breathe in as deeply and as slowly as you can. Then exhale as

# The Preferred Beverage for Monks Throughout the World

The monks of the Chinese Ch'an sect of Buddhists believed that the first cup of tea helped to keep a calm and clear mind while they sat in meditation. The second cup helped them feel as if the spirit was cleansed by the gentle rain. After a third cup, one can understand the nature of things.
—Anecdotal saying

As the popularity of tea grew in ancient China and moved on to Japan and other points in Asia, monks not only began to drink tea but also to save the seeds of the tea tree and carry them to each new destination, planting and harvesting them and then processing them into tea. The monks welcomed tea because it could relax the body while keeping the mind alert: two critical ingredients for long periods of contemplation and meditation. Soon tea became the preferred beverage for monks throughout the world. And even today, the monastic world celebrates tea for its ability to heighten awareness and bestow peace on all those willing to bring time and attention to its preparation.

deeply and as slowly as you can. Keep doing this until you feel connected with your breath; then open your eyes and, coming to a sitting position if you weren't already, sit still for a few moments or minutes. Accept whatever thoughts and feelings surface, and make a note of them mentally or write them down.

When you feel ready, arise slowly. Start to prepare your tea, and focus your attention entirely on doing that. As you make your tea, notice how more aware you feel after your relaxation and breathing. The leaves, the cup, the kettle, the steam—everything will appear

sharper, clearer, and more intense. You'll also be able to brew your tea with patience and to give it the concentration it deserves. And you will be able to drink it more slowly and savor the flavor, the aroma, and the taste more fully and with more pleasure than before.

When you have finished your tea, rinse out your cup and clean up. You will discover that you have greater energy and awareness after your short vacation of quiet meditation with tea.

## Meditate with tea every day

To reap the greatest reward, you should try to meditate with tea at least once a day. Make an appointment with yourself to get used to regular quiet, reflective time. Do your breathing exercise, let your mind wander, and then make a cup of tea with awareness. You may choose to include other meditation exercises before or after making your tea, like the ones listed in the box, but the important thing is that you give yourself this gift of quiet, reflective time.

> *Drink your tea slowly and reverently as if it is the axis on which the whole world revolves—slowly, evenly, without rushing toward the future. Live in the actual moment. Only this moment is life.*
> —Thich Nhat Hanh (1926–    ), Vietnamese-born Buddhist monk and author

## Who Looks Outside Dreams, Who Looks Inside Awakens

Meditation can be one of the most nourishing of companions, allowing us to dip into our inner selves, awaken our senses, and quench our spirits. Combining meditation with the joy of tea will only enhance the experience as you invite good feelings, love, or awareness into your being and you go to a place of stillness and calm that can fuel your body and quiet your mind.

# Meditation Exercises

## Breathing

Focusing on the breath is one of the most common and fundamental techniques for accessing the meditative state. Breath is a deep rhythm of the body that connects us intimately with the world around us.

Close your eyes, breathe deeply and regularly, and observe your breath as it flows into and out of your body. Give your full attention to the breath as it comes in, and full attention to the breath as it goes out. Whenever you find your attention wandering away from your breath, gently pull it back to the rising and falling of the breath.

Inhale through your nose slowly and deeply, feeling the lower chest and abdomen inflate like a balloon. Hold for five seconds. Exhale deeply, deflating the lower chest and abdomen like a balloon. Hold for five seconds. Do this three or four times, then allow your breathing to return to a normal rhythm.

You will begin to feel a change come over your entire body. Gradually you will become less aware of your breathing, but not captured in your stream of thoughts. You will become more centered inward. You will just "be there."

## Alternate Nostril Breathing

To alternate nostril breathing, you breathe in one nostril and exhale out of the other. To help get you started, gently place your right forefinger on your right nostril and inhale through your left nostril, using a count of four to slow down the inhale. Then exhale from your left nostril for the count of four. The left nostril is particularly important as it can help de-stress and relax you. Next, place your left forefinger on your left nostril and inhale through your right nostril for a count of four, then exhale from your right nostril for a count of four. Do not rush. Try to inhale and exhale slowly. Repeat until you feel a calm coming over you.

*continued*

## Listening

Sound entrains us in the busy world, but it also whispers of breeze and birds and children playing.

Close your eyes, breathe deeply and regularly, and separate from the chatter of the thought stream that flows through your mind. As your mind quiets and you relax, become aware of the variety of sounds that surround you. There is no need to do anything but listen. Listen with your ears; listen with your heart.

Let your focus gently float among the sounds of the world. Gradually you will flow inward, toward your center. Eventually you will not hear anything.

## Deep Centering

This exercise involves going into the very center of your being.

Close your eyes, breathe deeply and regularly, and imagine that you are going deep, deep into a well within your center. Visualize that this beautiful, deep well goes infinitely down and down. Breathe in as you descend, and absorb all the cool, soothing, healing energy that is buried deep in this bountiful well. Breathe out as you descend, and expel all the negative thoughts and energy that you have accumulated during your day.

Your deep inner world has its own essence, its own reality, its own light. Feel the silence, peace, and calm; no noise can reach you here, no words, no sound. Breathe deeply and slowly, experiencing your deepest, most serene essence in the silence of your deep well.

## Connecting

This exercise provides balance and connection upward and downward.

Close your eyes, and breathe deeply and regularly. Visualize clean white light pouring from above down into the top of your head, down through your body, and out your feet into the center of the Earth. As the light flows through you, allow it to illuminate and cleanse every cell of your body. Imagine every cell bright and alive with light.

Visualize bright clear emerald light coming up from the Earth, into your feet, up your legs, up your back, out the top of your head. Allow it to swirl through every cell, healing and nourishing and connecting you intimately to the very core of the Earth, of which you are a part.

Now allow both lights to flow through you, white from above and green from below, and combine them in a bright blend throughout your being.

Feel the connection to the Earth and the heavens, feel the calm nourishment of the energy, feel that the universe is truly your home.

### Your Natural Home

Home is where the heart is, and you will find this home in your heart.

Close your eyes, and breathe deeply and regularly. Imagine yourself in a beautiful, natural place among the mountain pines, on a deserted beach, in a spring meadow—anywhere you feel surrounded by the glory of nature.

Sit or recline comfortably, feeling absolutely safe and peaceful, and feel the gentle loving strength of the Earth beneath your body. Notice the fragrances and the sounds, feel the gentle breeze on your face. Let your eyes wander about, taking in the beauty of the trees, the birds, and the clouds.

Let your attention roam gently, appreciating the wonder of the environment around you. Settle into a deep appreciation that you are a part of all the glory of nature.

This place is your sanctuary, available to you anytime, through meditation or just a thought.

### Mantra

Whether spoken or not, words and sounds have vibrations, which can be conducive to meditation.

Close your eyes, and breathe deeply and regularly. Focus on a word or phrase that has meaning to you. It could be a mantra, a name, or a concept that has special power or significance.

Repeat the word in your mind with each exhalation. When your mind wanders, gently return it to the word as it repeats with your breath.

# Nourishing Blend № 10
## cultivate the tea mind

About Tea: Tea is more than just a sublime beverage; when savored with a tea mind, it becomes a brew that is rich in spiritual sustenance.

About Life: Satisfy the spirits in your life.

"The Way of Tea is based on the simple act of boiling water, making tea, offering it to others, and drinking of it ourselves. Served with a respectful heart and received with gratitude, a bowl of tea satisfies both physical and spiritual thirst," writes Urasenke, grand tea master of Sen Soshitsu XV.

The Japanese tea ceremony is designed to enrich both body and soul and elevates tea drinking to the realm of the spiritual, but you don't need to visit Japan or China or study tea ceremonies or even become a tea expert to cultivate the tea mind. As you'll see in this chapter, there are many ways to awaken your soul, satisfy the spirits in your life, and cultivate the tea mind.

*Tea is a religion of the art of life.*
—Katuzo Okakura (1862-1913), Japanese writer

## Brewing Your Own Spiritual Sustenance

Cultivating the tea mind means becoming aware of the beauty of things impermanent, imperfect, and incomplete. The simple act of making and serving tea becomes a symbol of this quest to find the spiritual in the ordinary and the everyday.

A tea master is someone who can prepare the perfect cup of tea with complete awareness and discipline, but making the perfect cup is a small part of the experience compared to the world of tranquility, respect, and honor she or he tries to create with the self, the guests, and the tea. Becoming a tea master entails years of practice and study—often a lifetime—and you might say that the delicacy of the tea ritual no longer fits into the often frenzied pace of Western life. But it is possible to slow down life and cultivate the tea mind, if only for a few moments.

To create a world of awareness, grace, and respect within your home, here are some suggestions for preparing both mind and tea.

### Preparing mind and tea

Create an environment that is clean, simple, fresh, and tranquil. By creating a clean, serene environment and serving your ware, you are offering yourself and your guests the best that you can.

Keep motion to a minimum while preparing your tea, and refrain from movements that have nothing to do with the preparation and serving of tea. If guests are present, prepare the tea while they are present. Making your tea mindfully is an expression of your appreciation for them and for the moment. To show respect to guests, use your finest tea, utensils, and crockery. Empty your mind of worry and idle chatter. Engage in pleasant conversation without rambling or jumping from one topic to another. At all times focus

on the preparation and enjoyment of the tea. In this way you are quieting your mind.

Always follow the soul-infusion guidelines in this book for water temperature, choice of tea leaves, and so forth. As you brew your tea, take time to savor the beautiful colors and shapes of the leaves, because appearance is very much part of the experience. If you are using a tea bag, focus your attention on something else pleasing—a vase of flowers, a tree outside your window, a ring, a necklace—it doesn't matter what as long as it's something that intrigues and inspires you. If you can't find anything to look at, focus your thoughts on something that inspires you.

## Awakening Your Soul

As we've seen throughout this book, a tea break means so much more than waiting for the kettle to boil. Tea has been called the plant of heaven, and for thousands of years it has been valued as a medicine, a drink of pleasure, and a drink to refresh the spirit. Taking time out for tea is about savoring the moment and focusing inward as well as on the tea.

Every time you drink tea, you will see different things. Every time you quiet your mind, you awaken your soul. Deep within us, permeating every cell, is the person we really are—our core, our soul, our essence. Your soul knows your potential and is constantly reminding you. When you feel empty or bored or not good enough, when shopping or worldly success don't lift you, when you feel depressed, it is time to awaken your soul. When you feel you have said the wrong thing to someone and want to go back and apologize, when you feel you have lost direction, when a relationship is not working, these are all soul nudges reminding you of your true potential. Whenever you are digging in the wrong place for happiness, your soul will let you know with messages of unhappiness, boredom, dissatisfaction. Listen to your soul; all your questions have an answer if you can learn to hear it. Discover what really drives you from within, and then match it with real-world activities to give your life purpose and meaning.

> *Its liquor is like the sweetest dew from heaven.*
> —Lu Yu (733–804), Chinese writer

## Reaching for Your Soul

Here's a beautiful way to contact your shining essence.

While waiting for your tea to brew, close your eyes and relax. Put your hand over your heart, and say to yourself, "I breathe the soul's breath." Exhale and then wait for your next breath to come naturally to you and fill your lungs. When your breath comes to you in this natural way, you are breathing the soul's breath. Repeat this exercise often, and do it with joy. Each time you do it, your soul contact will grow stronger.

Your soul is always waiting for your awareness so that it can inject your life again with clarity, meaning, and joy. Savor and appreciate your tea—and your life. In everything you feel, think, and do, no matter how ordinary, feel your soul breathing, and touch your shining essence.

> *Thank God for tea! What would the world do without tea!*
> *How did it exist? I am glad I was not born before tea.*
> —William Gladstone (1809–1898), British prime minister

# Afterword

Now that you've seen that a cup of tea is so much more than water and leaves or tea bags, I hope you'll never think of a cup of tea in the same way again. I also hope that you'll never look at a chipped mug, the branch of a tree, a well-read book, a bowl of steaming soup, a bunch of flowers, or anything else in the same way again. The English poet William Blake saw the world in a blade of grass, so why not see it in all the ordinary, everyday things that surround you? Why not find comfort, inspiration, and wonder in every aspect of your daily life, even the ordinary, the jaded, and the mundane?

Everything that exists has a soul, and everything in our lives is connected by that soul. Hard to believe? Modern physicists are beginning to discover that Western science and Eastern mysticism share a similar vision. In both scientific and mystical thought we are indeed all connected in the great web of life; we share universal energy in every breath, in every cup of tea; we *are* universal energy. Everything that exists contains the spark of universal energy—consciousness, God, divinity, spirit, intuition, soul, or whatever you choose to call it. When you can acknowledge the interconnectedness of all people and all things, you begin your spiritual journey. When you understand that we all share this eternal spark and that every creature in the universe, including our worst enemy, and everything in the universe, from your cup of tea to the stars in the sky, is connected, your soul begins to awaken.

Learning to connect with your spiritual energy is an ongoing and lifelong process, and there will be days when negativity closes down your true perceptions, but the more you take time to slow down and cultivate your awareness of the interconnectedness of all things, the easier it becomes to make the connection. At first it may seem a bit strained and you may feel full of doubt about what you are sensing, so take it slow—one tea break at a time—and don't take it too seriously. Remember, laughter also comes from your soul. Try not to analyze your spiritual experiences too much; just value and appreciate them, and the rewards will far exceed your expectations.

When you appreciate greatly and start to trust your spirit, your whole world will respond. So why not slow the pace a little, put the kettle on, and hitch your wagon to the stars? Your spiritual journey has begun.

*In the taste of a single cup of tea you will eventually discover the truth of all ten thousand forms of the universe.*
—Kyongbong Sunim, Ch'an (Zen) master

*Pour me a little more tea, would you, dear? I can drink it till it comes out of my ears.*
—Garek, *Star Trek: Deep Space 9*

# About the Author

Theresa Cheung writes full time and is the author of more than a dozen books, including *The Element Encyclopedia of Dreams, The Lazy Person's Guide to Stress,* as well as *Coffee Wisdom* and *Better than Sex: Chocolate Principles to Live By.* She has contributed to *Red, Prima,* and *She.* She lives in London, England.

# To Our Readers

Conari Press, an imprint of Red Wheel/Weiser, publishes books on topics ranging from spirituality, personal growth, and relationships to women's issues, parenting, and social issues. Our mission is to publish quality books that will make a difference in people's live—how we feel about ourselves and how we relate to one another. We value integrity, compassion, and receptivity, both in the books we publish and in the way we do business.

Our readers are our most important resource, and we value your input, suggestions, and ideas about what you would like to see published. Please feel free to contact us, to request our latest book catalog, or to be added to our mailing list.

Conari Press
An imprint of Red Wheel/Weiser, LLC
500 Third Street, Suite 230
San Francisco, CA 94107
*www.redwheelweiser.com*